Fear of the Evil Eye

"Safia Yun has written an essential work on an understudied area of Islamic folk belief: the evil eye. This work combines historical background with fascinating interviews with contemporary Jordanian Muslim women. I highly recommend this work to anyone doing ministry among Muslims."

—R. DON DEAL,
director of classical apologetics,
Norman Geisler International Ministries

"The custom related to the Evil Eye has long been a deeply rooted religious practice in the Muslim world, especially in the lives of Muslim women. This work is based on in-depth interviews with young women in Jordan, including university students, and provides a detailed analysis of how this custom has impacted their lives, particularly their social relationships with acquaintances. Such lived experiences solidify the credibility of the study. It does not merely emphasize the negative worldview of this custom but also proposes a missionary approach to prevent its resulting negative effects through the practice of giving mutual compliments. This helps remind individuals of God's grace and blessings towards each other, rather than fostering mutual rejection and hatred. It is a meaningful work that suggests transforming curses into expressions of gratitude for blessings, offering a beautiful missionary application."

—AH YOUNG KIM,
professor, Torch Trinity Graduate University, Seoul

"As a colleague of Safia Yun for several years in India, I learned with great interest of her new work *Fear of the Evil Eye*. It is based on her field research and life among Jordanian Muslim women, and connections between the Evil Eye and envy. The sensitivity and attention to context I saw in Yun's work in India is also evidenced here. It is an important resource for ministry not only in the Middle East but beyond."

—STEVE COCHRANE,
Youth With a Mission, University of the Nations

"An insightful exploration of the evil eye and a rich engagement with its contemporary practice among young Muslim women in Jordan! Far from being just a folkloric symbol, the belief in the evil eye is deeply ingrained in the lives of people, reflecting the spiritual and emotional needs of individuals and societies. This research offers readers a deeper understanding of modern folk practices and provides insights on how to engage with people through God's abundant blessings."

—SAM KIM,
assistant professor of intercultural studies,
School of Christian Studies, Asbury University

"While there have been many academic and scholarly books written concerning ministry and mission in the context of Muslim communities, few of these have sought to address issues of folk beliefs and folk religion. Addressing these, however, is often crucial not only in communicating the gospel initially, but in the context of discipleship and building communities of faithful followers of Jesus. In *Fear of the Evil Eye*, Safia Yun addresses one of the most hidden, yet persistent issues across Muslim communities, with a heart to seeing women in these communities set free from such fear into the freedom they will find in Jesus. Though she addresses these within the specific context of her interaction with Jordanian women, much of how she addresses this will have a wider application. Practitioners and scholars alike would do well to include this in their reading for a grounded understanding and practical wisdom in addressing this topic."

—MATTHEW FRIEDMAN,
affiliate professor, Asbury Theological Seminary

Fear of the Evil Eye

A Missional Approach Toward the Envious Gaze Among Young Jordanian Muslim Women

SAFIA J. YUN

Foreword by Warren Larson

WIPF & STOCK · Eugene, Oregon

FEAR OF THE EVIL EYE
A Missional Approach Toward the Envious Gaze Among Young Jordanian Muslim Women

Copyright © 2025 Safia J. Yun. All rights reserved. Except for brief quotations in critical publications or reviews, no part of this book may be reproduced in any manner without prior written permission from the publisher. Write: Permissions, Wipf and Stock Publishers, 199 W. 8th Ave., Suite 3, Eugene, OR 97401.

Wipf & Stock
An Imprint of Wipf and Stock Publishers
199 W. 8th Ave., Suite 3
Eugene, OR 97401

www.wipfandstock.com

PAPERBACK ISBN: 979-8-3852-3543-8
HARDCOVER ISBN: 979-8-3852-3544-5
EBOOK ISBN: 979-8-3852-3545-2

VERSION NUMBER 01/16/25

Scripture quotations are from the Authorized (King James) Version. Rights in the Authorized Version in the United Kingdom are vested in the Crown. Reproduced by permission of the Crown's patentee, Cambridge University Press. Emphases added.

Scripture quotations are from the ESV® Bible (The Holy Bible, English Standard Version®), © 2001 by Crossway, a publishing ministry of Good News Publishers. Used by permission. All rights reserved. The ESV text may not be quoted in any publication made available to the public by a Creative Commons license. The ESV may not be translated in whole or in part into any other language.

Contents

List of Tables | vi

Foreword by Warren Larson | vii

Acknowledgments | xi

Abbreviations | xiii

Introduction | xv

1   Evil Eye Belief and Practice | 1

2   Biblical and Qur'anic Perspectives | 21

3   Narratives of Young Jordanian Muslim Women | 40

4   Missional Implications and Approaches | 73

5   Conclusion | 94

Bibliography | 97

List of Tables

Table 1. Causes of the Evil Eye | 46
Table 2. Methods of Protection and Cure | 67

Foreword

THIS BOOK IS ABOUT FOLK Islam in Jordan, but the implications reach all across the Middle East and beyond. Safia Yun interviewed sixty women in five cities across Jordan, fifty-eight of whom believe anyone potentially can have the evil eye. These women affirm that whoever possesses such power can cause harm to flocks, crops, property, and humans, and can even rob people of their sleep. It springs from envy, they say, and is so deeply embedded in the culture that the word for "eye" (*ayn*) and the word for "envy" (*hasad*) are used interchangeably. In other words, "I must have what he/she has, or I want him/her not to have what I deeply value." A person avoids giving compliments, as a precaution from giving anyone the idea they are envious and possess the evil eye. If a compliment is unavoidable, a quick *Mashallah* (God willed it) is appropriate to ensure there is no evil intended.

Significantly, interviewees in this study are young, college-educated women, who previously have been left out of such research on the evil eye. It is "unfamiliar ground." One might assume that only the older generation would cling to antiquated beliefs like the evil eye, but the average age of these women is twenty-five. Regardless of age, the most damage takes place among people who know each other best. It fosters fear and can easily ruin relationships among family and friends. In addition, it can cause mental problems, and rob people of their security, joy, and peace. It also creates secrecy and suspicion through a practice called *kitman*.

FOREWORD

When I'm about to do something, I don't tell anyone; I just do it and tell others later.

The author gives examples of how this plays out. In one case, a woman's brother had purchased a car, but after three accidents, she concluded it was because of the evil eye. Many had seen the car, had good reason to be envious, and so someone chose to inflict harm. In another case, a young woman had purchased a wedding dress, but when she went to pick it up, the shopkeeper had sold it to someone else. Obviously, envy was the cause, otherwise it would not have happened. When bad things happen, questions surface: Why did I fail? Why can't I have children? Why am I sick? Why did this tragedy happen? Why did my daughter die? Why does my hair fall out? Why do I have pimples? All of these bad things occur because of the evil eye. These young women are simply trying to get on in life, but are being hindered and held down by the evil eye.

These interviewees' responses are quite different from how their mothers might have reacted. Unlike their mothers, who would have used amulets for protection, these women use the Qur'an and Hadith as a remedy. In this way, Yun shows that we cannot presume to know the practices of any segment of society without doing fresh research. Amulets are currently sold in Jordan, but only secretly. By using the Qur'an, these young women can claim orthodoxy in a conservative society. After all, according to the Hadith, this is how Muhammad dealt with the evil eye. The "two protectors" in the Qur'an (Surahs 113 and 114) can be recited when needed. In fact, these short passages are often memorized. Other portions of the Qur'an may be written out on bits and pieces of paper to guard against harm and danger. The Qur'an is used as a powerful tool, not only to protect from evil but to cure wrongs.

In the end, Yun gives a strong call for Christian mission that includes special training. One half of those interviewed said they had seen/experienced harm from a relative or a friend, so there is a desperate need for truth and light to shine where the evil eye reigns supreme. The author argues that Christian workers cannot effectively minister unless they know the root of the problem. Sin and selfishness must be confronted. The young women admit that the evil eye springs from an unclean heart, so this is a good place to start. Ministry is not just a matter of engaging Islam, but of meeting Muslims where they are. Workers must bring Jesus into each setting and boldly pray in his powerful name. They must understand the context of the people in order to effectively share the gospel.

Moreover, sharing the gospel must include a discussion of who God is. Muslims use the expression *Allah Kareem* (God is generous), but few understand it. The truth is, he is a gracious, generous, and giving God, who does not begrudge us of blessings. The author highlights that the word *baraka* (blessing) is found 369 times in the Hebrew Bible, so Christian workers must make much of God as the blesser, and they must model his kindness and generosity at all times. The good news is that Jesus is more than able to protect us from every harm and danger, including the evil eye. Those who follow him can say, "I am content because of what God has given me."

The overarching message of this book is that sin divides, but the cross unites. Satan sows discord, suspicion, and fear, but Jesus gives peace and brings us together: "God, who reconciled us to himself through Christ gave us the ministry of reconciliation" (2 Cor 5:18).

> Warren Larson, PhD
> *Senior Research Fellow and Professor*
> College of Intercultural Studies
> Columbia International University

Acknowledgments

NO FRUIT IS BORNE without patience and pain. My deep gratitude goes to Dr. Warren Larson, who has walked with me throughout my research until this book came out amid his own pain and grief.

Abbreviations

BECNT	Baker Exegetical Commentary on the New Testament
BibInt	*Biblical Interpretation*
CBQ	*Catholic Biblical Quarterly*
CurTM	*Currents in Theology and Mission*
DBS	Discovery Bible Study
ICC	International Critical Commentary
IJFM	*International Journal of Frontier Missions*
JBL	*Journal of Biblical Literature*
JNES	*Journal of Near Eastern Studies*
LCL	Loeb Classical Library
Neot	*Neotestamentica*
NICNT	New International Commentary on the New Testament
StPohl	Studia Pohl
SWBA	Social World of Biblical Antiquity
TNTC	Tyndale New Testament Commentaries
TOTC	Tyndale Old Testament Commentaries
WUNT	Wissenschaftliche Untersuchungen zum Neuen Testament

Introduction

WHEN I FIRST ARRIVED in Jordan, one of the earliest cultural lessons I learned was the significance of compliments. Complimenting another woman's clothing or jewelry often results in her offering the item to me as a gift. This gesture stems from a fear of envy and the belief that the envious eye might bring harm. To avoid such damage, it's customary to use the phrase *Mashallah* (ما شاء الله), meaning "Allah has willed it," which is understood as invoking protection against the evil eye.

With over two decades of experience living in various cultures, particularly among Muslims, I've continuously learned new cultural norms and beliefs, often experiencing culture shock. My previous experiences with Muslims in India provided a foundation for my transition to life in Jordan. Over the past six years, while learning Arabic and the local culture, I've discovered deeply held beliefs and widespread practices among Arab Muslim women. Some of these beliefs are familiar from other Muslim contexts, while others are unique to Jordan.

In Jordan, the concept of envy (حسد, *hasad*), often interchanged with the term for the evil eye, is pervasive. When someone compliments an item in a Jordanian household, the owner typically offers it as a gift to prevent harm from the envious eye. Though the proper response is to decline the offer, the act of offering underscores the fear of envy and the evil eye.

Envy frequently surfaces in conversations among friends and colleagues. For instance, a Jordanian neighbor recently shared her workplace stress, attributing it to envy and competition among colleagues. Despite her discomfort with the atmosphere envy creates, she acknowledged its omnipresence in Jordanian society.

For many Jordanian Muslim women, beliefs related to the evil eye and envy give rise to fear. Fear is not restricted to any individual or culture. On the contrary, it is a universal emotion among humans and exists in all cultures and religions. However, fear seems to control people's lives here in Jordan. They are afraid of an envious look or the evil eye, what people might say, and losing honor or being shamed. Often, these fears are not so much on an individual but on a communal level. As fear of envious looks (the evil eye) permeates relationships in Jordan, it is clear that envy represents a significant cultural characteristic of Jordanian society.

The belief in the evil eye dates back to the ancient Mediterranean world, where it was thought that certain people could cause harm with a mere look. This belief has spread across various cultures and remains strong among Muslims in the Middle East. The evil eye is feared for the misfortunes it is believed to bring, from health issues to crop failures, and is often associated with envy.

In everyday life, the evil eye is a common topic of conversation. I've overheard taxi drivers mentioning it and women jokingly denying they've cast it. This deep-rooted belief significantly influences people's thoughts and behaviors.

Despite its prevalence, the concept of the evil eye can be unfamiliar to expatriates and cross-cultural workers. For example, while riding with a Jordanian friend and an American friend, I noticed old shoes hanging from an electric line—a local practice to ward off the evil eye. My Jordanian friend explained its purpose, while the American, despite having lived in Jordan for years, was unaware of this practice. This highlighted a gap in understanding among some expatriates regarding local beliefs and practices.

My initial exposure to the evil eye was in India, but in Jordan, I sensed pervasiveness and felt urged to delve deeper into this belief. My research aims to understand how the evil eye affects the lives and relationships of young Muslim women in Jordan. By examining biblical and Qur'anic perspectives and interpreting narratives

INTRODUCTION

from local women, I hope to provide insights for cross-cultural workers to better understand and engage with these beliefs.

Understanding the belief in the evil eye among Jordanian Muslim women is crucial for anyone working in this cultural context. My research seeks to illuminate the complexities of this belief and its impact on daily life, providing a foundation for more effective cross-cultural interactions and support.

RATIONALE AND NEED FOR STUDY

Despite its prevalence, there is a lack of scholarly research on the evil eye in contemporary Middle Eastern sociocultural and religious contexts, particularly among younger Muslim women. This study aims to fill that gap by focusing on young Jordanian Muslim women and their beliefs, expressions, and practices related to the evil eye. It seeks to examine how these beliefs influence their thoughts and actions.

Most existing research on the evil eye is based on ancient literature, including Egyptian and Greek texts, which provides valuable insights into the worldview of ancient peoples. The belief in the evil eye spread widely, influencing many cultures and religions, including the three major monotheistic faiths of the Mediterranean region.

However, studies examining the evil eye from a biblical or Islamic perspective are rare. Understanding what the Bible says about the evil eye in its sociocultural and economic contexts can shed light on how Hebrews and early Christians understood and dealt with this concept. A biblical perspective helps deepen our understanding of the evil eye complex, particularly in community settings.

Similarly, exploring what Islam teaches about the evil eye and how Muslims perceive and practice related beliefs is crucial. Since the notion of the evil eye is prevalent among Arab Muslims, further exploration from an Islamic perspective is valuable for those working in this context. This study aims to understand how young Muslim women in Jordan and the Middle East perceive the evil eye today and to find relevant implications and approaches for this specific group.

The goal of this study is to benefit students of missions and cross-cultural workers among Arabs, particularly Arab Muslim women. By clarifying the evil eye complex and how it works, cross-cultural workers can gain confidence in addressing it. A thorough understanding of the subject can prevent preconceptions and insufficient knowledge from hindering discussions and necessary actions. Knowledge of both biblical teachings and local beliefs about the evil eye will aid cross-cultural workers in their ministry in the Middle East and beyond.

This study also aims to benefit trainers and leaders of mission agencies. By equipping students of missions and new cross-cultural workers with knowledge about popular or folk beliefs and practices, these leaders can enhance the effectiveness of their ministries among Muslim women.

Finally, this study hopes to benefit Arab Muslim women themselves. As cross-cultural workers engage with local Muslim women with better understanding, these women can gain new perspectives and insights as they confront their beliefs and fears.

Focusing on a younger generation of Muslim women in Jordan, this study examines how they perceive and deal with the evil eye and how these beliefs affect their behaviors, relationships, and social life. The research does not assume that younger women hold the same perceptions or observe the same practices as the older generation. By comparing ancient beliefs with modern understandings among educated young Jordanian Muslim women and college students, this study addresses a significant gap in scholarly research related to the evil eye, particularly in terms of Muslim women's perceptions and practices and the belief system's influence on their society and spiritual lives.

RESEARCH QUESTIONS

To understand young Jordanian Muslim women's perceptions and experiences with the evil eye, I seek to answer several questions:

INTRODUCTION

1. How do young Jordanian Muslim women understand the evil eye in terms of their experiences, Islamic religion, and Arabic cultural teachings?

This question explores their general and experiential knowledge of the evil eye, including its causes, effects, and the various occasions on which it manifests. It also examines their understanding of the evil eye from religious, social, and cultural perspectives. In Jordan, Islamic religion and culture are deeply intertwined. Therefore, this question emphasizes what Jordanian Muslim women know about the evil eye from Islam and how they believe it influences their culture as a whole.

2. How does the evil eye affect the lives and relationships of young Muslim women in Jordan?

This question investigates how young women feel about the evil eye and how it impacts their relationships with others. The research assumes that belief in and fear of the evil eye primarily affect the women themselves and, secondarily, their relationships with other women. It aims to draw out their feelings and the relational dynamics influenced by the evil eye.

3. What methods do young Muslim women in Jordan use to protect themselves from the evil eye?

Many Arabs live in fear of the evil eye, and there are various known protective measures and cures among Arab Muslims, which may vary according to religious status and cultural and family influences. This question explores how younger women seek to protect themselves from the evil eye's harm by revealing their beliefs, mindsets, and popular practices.

4. What are the missional implications based on young Jordanian Muslim women's beliefs in the evil eye?

This question seeks to identify missional implications and relevant approaches to ministering to a younger generation of Muslim women who believe in and are afraid of the evil eye. It aims to suggest effective strategies for engaging with and supporting these women in light of their beliefs.

Introduction

SCOPE AND DELIMITATIONS

This study is limited to examining the beliefs and practices related to the evil eye among young Muslim women in Jordan. It does not address other beliefs and practices, such as black magic, witchcraft, jinn, sorcery, evil spirits, or Satan. While popular or folk Islamic beliefs and practices are valuable to study, this research focuses solely on the evil eye.

The scope includes university students and young Muslim women in their twenties and thirties in Jordan. In Arab societies, the belief in the evil eye is deeply ingrained and has been passed down through generations. Although the older generation is more rooted in these traditions, this study focuses on the younger generation to explore how their beliefs and practices compare.

The participants were educated Muslim women, half of whom were current university students and the rest of whom were recent graduates. The deliberate choice of educated young women aims to determine if higher education influences their beliefs and practices related to the evil eye, and how these might differ from those of the older, more traditional generation. This focus on educated younger women provides contemporary insights into the perception of the evil eye among the younger generation.

The study is further limited to Jordanian Muslim women and does not include Arab Christian women. While the belief in the evil eye is common across all three monotheistic religions, focusing on Muslim women allows for a more detailed and specific analysis. By concentrating on one ethno-religious group, the study ensures precise data findings that can yield relevant implications.

Despite the narrow scope, the results of this study may have broader applications for other Muslim women in another region and provide valuable insights for understanding the evil eye belief among younger, educated Muslim women in Jordan.

Introduction

DEFINITION OF KEY TERMS

- Arab: An individual whose native language is Arabic. Modern usage includes any Arabic-speaking peoples living in the vast region from Mauritania, on the Atlantic coast of Africa, to southwestern Iran, encompassing the entire Maghreb of North Africa, Egypt and Sudan, the Arabian Peninsula, and Syria and Iraq. It is incorrect to say that all Arabs are Muslims; Arabs can be Christians and belong to other religious groups. This study focuses specifically on Arab Muslim women in Jordan, not Arab Christian women.

- Envy: A feeling of resentment and displeasure arising from observing another person's superiority in happiness, success, reputation, or the possession of something desirable, coupled with the wish that the person be deprived of that asset. This differs from jealousy, which is the fear of losing something to others, although the two terms are often used interchangeably in modern language.

- Evil eye: An envious look believed to cause harm. The evil eye is prevalent in many parts of the world and is the belief that certain individuals can inflict harm through a mere envious gaze or by praising an object or its owner.

- *Mashallah* (ما شاء الله): An Arabic phrase that translates to "what Allah has willed happened," "Allah has willed it." It can also mean "May Allah protect you." The phrase expresses appreciation and praise and invokes Allah's protection against the evil eye.

- Jinn: The word in Arabic refers to something that is covered or concealed. Jinn refers to the spiritual forces or beings that live among man but cannot be seen. A connotation includes satanic forces as well as angels and angelic forces since all of them are concealed from human senses. The Qur'an states that the jinn were created from a smokeless flame of fire or out of the scorching fire. Jinn have free will to choose like

INTRODUCTION

human beings. Among the jinn, there are those who are obedient to God and others who are not.

- Sheikh: A religious leader who knows the Qur'an well and solves problems in people's lives; can also mean a witch doctor who heals against witchcraft/illness, etc.

1

Evil Eye Belief and Practice

THE CONCEPT OF THE evil eye is ancient and widespread across numerous cultures. It affects millions worldwide, with anecdotes readily available from individuals of diverse backgrounds. Understanding the evil eye is crucial for comprehending its significance in the lives of Jordanian Muslim women, explored in later chapters. This section begins by defining the evil eye and describing its historical and cultural contexts. It also examines various preventive methods and cures found across different cultures, followed by an evaluation of scholarly perspectives on this phenomenon.

DEFINITION AND DESCRIPTION

The evil eye refers to the belief that certain individuals possess a gaze capable of causing harm or misfortune to others, including illness or damage to possessions. This belief spans various cultures and historical periods, attributing power to envy-ridden looks or spoken words. It's believed to affect vulnerable groups like nursing mothers, children, and those deemed successful or attractive. The evil eye can be intentional, rooted in malice, or unintentional, arising from envy or admiration. Protective measures against it range from religious artifacts like the Eye of Horus to folk practices such as wearing amulets or performing specific gestures. This belief is reflected in ancient texts and artifacts worldwide, highlighting its geographical and cultural prevalence.

The term "evil eye" appears across different languages and cultures, such as *ophthalmos ponéros* and *baskania* in Greek, *böser Blick* in German, *ra' ayn* in Hebrew, and *ayn* or *hasad* in Arabic, where it directly translates as "envy." The Latin equivalent is *fascinatio*, which translates as *fascination*, the original meaning of which is to bewitch or to injure with an evil eye. This belief has persisted for millennia, with references dating back to ancient Sumeria around 3,000 BC. It spread from Mesopotamia through the Mediterranean and beyond, influencing cultures in Europe, Asia, and the Americas.

The belief in the evil eye, also known as *fascination*, is found in many nations' literature. As William W. Story describes, "It has numbered among its adherents—poets and lawgivers, emperors, and slaves, learned men and savages, philosophers, and fools. It has been vainly derived by science, abjured by religion, and prohibited by law."[1]

The Hebrews were well acquainted with the evil eye, which is mentioned in the Old and New Testaments of the Bible. Solomon, in his wisdom, warns, "Eat thou not the bread of him that hath an evil eye" (Prov 23:6). Jesus, in his Sermon on the Mount, speaks, "But if thine eye be evil, thy whole body shall be full of darkness" (Matt 6:23). The apostle Paul rebukes, "O foolish Galatians, who hath bewitched you?" (Gal 3:1), which uses the metaphor of the evil eye to bewitch. The evil eye is also alluded to in the Qur'an (Surah 113, Al-Falaq) as the neighbor's envy through an evil eye. The Hadiths (sayings of Prophet Muhammad) contain many references related to it. Muslims firmly believe in the evil eye's existence and pray this surah for protection. The terms for the evil eye and envy are interchangeable in Arabic. Thus, three monotheistic religions in the circum-Mediterranean and the Middle East share the evil eye belief, though their understanding of it differs.

In the discussion of the evil eye belief, it is vital to note that the prevalent view in antiquity held that the eye was an active

---

1. Story, *Castle St. Angelo*, 147.

EVIL EYE BELIEF AND PRACTICE

organ projecting particles of energy and light. This view remained dominant through late antiquity and the Middle Ages. The eye was considered the caster of light, which the eye saw by projecting something on the object of regard.[2] Hence, the ancient Mediterranean world believed that the evil eye was associated with envy aroused from within, which caused harm to its victims through an envious gaze. Very often, evil eye and envy are used interchangeably and related closely. The eye was regarded as a conveyor of emotions, especially envy. Envy was among the most feared, despised, and condemned vices.[3] Further, it was thought that envy expresses displeasure and resentment of the heart toward the good fortunes of others.

EVIL EYE BELIEF AND PRACTICE FROM ANCIENT TO PRESENT

Evidence of the evil eye belief spans from ancient Mesopotamia to contemporary societies. Literary texts, artifacts, and archaeological discoveries from various cultures demonstrate its enduring presence. This section traces its origins in Mesopotamia and its adoption in Egypt, Greece, and Rome, exploring its evolution into contemporary Islamic and folk practices.

Mesopotamia and Egypt

The concept of the evil eye originated in ancient Sumeria, evidenced by cuneiform texts dating back to the third millennium BC. Sumerians believed in malevolent spirits capable of cursing individuals and their possessions, leading them to develop protective charms and incantations. Excavations at sites like Tell Brak in Syria reveal thousands of "eye idols," likely used to ward off the evil

---

2. Potts, *World's Eye*, 5; Elliott explains the "extramission theory of vision" in detail (*Beware the Evil Eye*, 2:78–100).

3. Elliott, *Beware the Evil Eye*, 1:118.

eye, particularly from vulnerable groups like infants and nursing mothers.

Primary evidence of the evil eye belief in ancient Mesopotamia comes from incantation texts. Graham Cunningham has cataloged 448 Mesopotamian incantations dating from 2500 to 1500 BC.[4] Throughout the Sumerian, Akkadian, and Old Babylonian periods, these incantations were directed against various dangers, including the evil eye. An Akkadian incantation from this era specifically highlights the threat posed by the evil eye to infants and mothers during childbirth, a recurring theme across centuries.

Another Sumerian-Babylonian incantation describes additional harms attributed to the evil eye: drought, harm to domestic animals and milk production, and afflictions upon young men and women. This incantation was intended to ward off all destructive forces, whether natural or demonic, including the personification of the evil eye as a demon, as noted by archaeologist R. Campbell Thompson in a Syriac charm.[5]

The content of these incantations underscores the widespread fear of the evil eye in Mesopotamia, persisting over centuries. Key aspects of the belief included viewing the evil eye as an active rather than passive force capable of harming any object with its glance. It was believed that anyone could possess the evil eye, often associated with colors such as blue and red, and connected closely with envy. Protective measures, including incantations, were believed to be effective in safeguarding against its effects, a pattern that would recur across cultures and centuries.

In ancient Egyptian culture, which shared agricultural roots and faced similar environmental challenges as Sumer and Babylonia, belief in the evil eye likely originated from Mesopotamia but developed uniquely in Egypt. The exact period of its emergence is debated, though myths and symbols like the Eye of Horus suggest its presence in early Egyptian history.

Abundant archaeological evidence indicates that ancient Egyptians held a strong belief in the evil eye and feared its effects.

---

4. Cunningham, *Deliver Me from Evil*.
5. Thompson, *Devils and Evil Spirits*.

Art, sculpture, and amulets, particularly found within tombs and coffins, demonstrate this belief. The Eye of Horus (*udjat* eye), represented as a stylized hawk eye with a feather pattern, served as a prominent protective amulet worn by both the living and the deceased. Initially a celestial symbol, the Eye of Horus later assumed a protective role against malevolent gazes, particularly those aimed at harming children and their health.

During Egypt's later periods under Greek and Roman influence (332 BC to late antiquity), a fusion of cultures occurred, spreading Egyptian beliefs, including those regarding the evil eye, throughout the Mediterranean region. This dissemination influenced subsequent beliefs among Greeks, Romans, Israelites, and early Christians, reflecting parallels with the Mesopotamian and Egyptian concepts of the evil eye.

Greece and Rome

Early traces of the evil eye belief can be found as far back as the era of Homer (eighth century BC). In the *Iliad*, Homer vividly describes an eye with anger and a potent killing glance: "Agamemnon, furious, his dark heart filled to the brim, blazing with anger now, his eyes like searing fire. With a sudden, killing look, he wheeled on Calchas first."[6] Here, the threatening gaze is metaphorically linked to the heart and its ability to harm and injure.

The Greeks and Romans embraced the belief in the evil eye wholeheartedly. The Greek verb *baskainein* meant "to kill with a glance of the eye," as evidenced in Greek literature using *bask-* root words, underscoring the widespread belief in this phenomenon. In Latin, this power was termed *fascinatio*, from which the English word "fascination" derives, rooted in the ancient concept of causing harm with an evil eye. The protective amulet against the evil eye often took the form of a phallus. This potent charm was widely recognized as the most effective safeguard against the evil eye in

---

6. Homer, *Iliad*, 1:102–5.

the Roman world, often worn around the necks of children until they reached adulthood.

Within the Greek-speaking Hellenistic world, personal letters commonly included wishes for recipients and their families to "remain unharmed by the evil eye" or "be kept safe from its influence." This practice was also evident in Christian papyri, reflecting a serious concern across religious boundaries.[7] Notably, the term *abasakantos* (safe from the evil eye) was even used as a personal name.[8]

Romans believed that anyone could possess the ability to cast the evil eye, with references in ancient sources to individuals who had a peculiar ocular trait known as *pupula duplex* (double pupil). Pliny the Elder, in his *Natural History* (AD 23/24–79), affirmed this belief, suggesting that those with double pupils could harm anything at which they glanced.[9] Romans attempted to rationalize the evil eye through physical attributes such as the double pupil, aligning with contemporary physiognomy theories that linked a person's character to their physical appearance.[10]

During Pliny's time, specific laws were enacted to hold accountable those believed to have used the evil eye to harm crops. Romans even attributed envy to their gods, believing that lesser gods could be envious and cast their malevolent gaze upon others.[11] Such beliefs were deeply ingrained in Roman culture, reflected in sayings like *Mantis te vidit* (Some fascinator has looked at you!) when a person fell ill without apparent cause.[12]

Among both Greeks and Romans, spitting was a common practice to ward off the evil eye. Greeks would spit three times at a child when complimenting them, accompanied by the words "May no evil come to you!" Similarly, Romans would spit on their chests

---

7. Elliott, *Beware the Evil Eye*, 2:1–24.
8. Elliott, *Beware the Evil Eye*, 2:37.
9. Pliny the Elder, *Natural History*, 7:16–18.
10. Nuño, "Ocular Pathologies," 304.
11. Park, *Evil Eye*, 12.
12. Story, *Castle St. Angelo*, 150–51.

as a protective gesture when praising others or to deny casting the evil eye, uttering "no evil eye intended" with each spit.

Contrary to the misconception that the belief in the evil eye was held only by the uneducated or peasants, evidence suggests that even educated elites were firm believers. Plutarch (AD 50–120), a prominent philosopher, discussed the evil eye in his *Symposium* (table talk), exploring its phenomenon, the extramission theory of vision, and its association with envy.[13] Discussions included the use of amulets believed to deflect envy and the operation of the evil eye, showing a rationalized understanding among the educated elite.

Scholars like John H. Elliott argue that for figures such as Plutarch and his peers, the evil eye was not merely superstition but a perceived physical reality explainable within the rational framework of their time. Envy, perceived as an outward projection triggered by witnessing others' good fortune, was believed to manifest through the eye. This link between envy and the evil eye was well established in Greek literature from the time of Demosthenes, Plato, Aristotle, Strabo, and Hellenistic poets onward.[14]

In summary, the beliefs surrounding the evil eye among Greeks and Romans inherited elements from Mesopotamian and Egyptian cultures. These beliefs portrayed the evil eye as an active force projecting harmful energy and light, based on contemporary scientific and logical frameworks. This belief persisted through late antiquity (c. AD 600) into the Middle Ages, portraying the evil eye as capable of striking victims with its powerful glance, often attributed to envy and feared by ancient societies who sought protection through various protective measures.

From Medieval Times to Today

The belief in the evil eye persisted from late antiquity through the Middle Ages and continues to influence cultures worldwide today.

---

13. *Quaestiones convivales* 5.7, in Plutarch, *Plutarch's "Moralia."*
14. Elliott, *Beware the Evil Eye*, 2:84–85.

Unlike many superstitions that faded over time, the belief in the evil eye remained robust throughout history, shaping everyday life across different eras.

During the Middle Ages, Renaissance, and Reformation, prominent figures such as Thomas Aquinas, Dante Alighieri, Leonardo da Vinci, Martin Luther, and Francis Bacon all acknowledged and discussed the concept of the evil eye. It was considered a potent force capable of causing calamities like plague, smallpox, and cholera. Serious treatises addressing the evil eye were written as late as the 1800s, underscoring its enduring significance.

In the eighteenth century, the evil eye became associated with witchcraft. During the Enlightenment, while witch beliefs were debated intensely, the evil eye was often depicted as a glaring or piercing eye associated with witches.[15] The *Malleus Maleficarum* (The hammer of witches, 1486), a pivotal text of the Inquisition, linked the evil eye directly to accusations of witchcraft, shaping perceptions and fears during that era.

Frederick T. Elworthy documented various witchcraft practices globally, illustrating how animals like horses, cows, and camels were believed to be vulnerable to the evil eye. In Scotland and England, it was believed that admiring glances from strangers could lead to illness or misfortune in livestock, a belief that persisted into the nineteenth century.[16]

Nicola Valletta, a professor of Roman jurisprudence, wrote extensively about the evil eye (*jettatura*), posing questions about its mechanics and effects that reflected common concerns of the time. His inquiries into whether certain individuals or groups were more susceptible to casting the evil eye reveal the depth of belief surrounding this phenomenon.[17]

Throughout the Age of Enlightenment and into modern times, beliefs and practices concerning infants, children, and the evil eye have persisted across cultures. In many societies, newborns, children, and nursing mothers are considered especially

---

15. Jones, "Evil Eye Among European-Americans," 152.
16. Elworthy, *Evil Eye*, 11.
17. Valletta, *Cicalata sul Fascino*.

susceptible to the evil eye. Protective measures vary widely, from marking children's faces in India to intentionally neglecting cleanliness in Iran to ward off envy.

In contemporary Middle Eastern societies, stories about the evil eye continue to appear in local newspapers and personal narratives. Many individuals take precautions such as reciting specific verses from the Qur'an, saying *Mashallah*, keeping achievements secret, or performing rituals like sprinkling water to counteract the perceived effects of envy.

The belief in the evil eye has adapted to modern contexts, reflecting both continuity and change. In Mediterranean cultures, an amulet known as *nazar* (blue-colored eye-shaped talisman) is widely used to ward off the evil eye, while in Latin America, red strings and other charms are common. These cultural artifacts demonstrate how traditional beliefs are integrated into contemporary life, often intersecting with local customs and religious practices.

Globalization has also played a role in the spread and transformation of the evil eye belief. With increased migration and cultural exchange, practices associated with the evil eye have crossed borders, influencing communities far from their origins. For example, the use of blue eye amulets has become popular in Western countries as a fashion accessory, sometimes divorced from its original protective connotations.

Despite scientific advancements and increased rationality in the modern world, the belief in the evil eye endures, highlighting the persistent human need to explain and mitigate misfortune through cultural and supernatural means.

Evil Eye in Islam

The belief in the evil eye holds a significant place within Islam, its origins deeply intertwined with the animistic practices prevalent among pagan Arabs before the advent of Islam in the seventh century. These practices encompassed beliefs in spiritual entities like jinn, witchcraft, magic, and the malevolent influence of the evil eye on human affairs. Despite Islam's proclamation of monotheism, these animistic elements were not entirely discarded but rather assimilated and transformed within its framework.

Pre-Islamic Arabian society invoked and worshipped jinn, as referenced in the Qur'an (Surahs 6:100; 34:41; 37:158). These beliefs persisted alongside the rise of Islam, where fear of harm from evil spirits and the evil eye was pervasive. Such fears were managed through rituals aimed at controlling these supernatural forces.

The influence of Jewish and early Christian communities in the circum-Mediterranean region also shaped Islamic beliefs regarding the evil eye. Though the Qur'an does not directly mention the evil eye, it indirectly references concepts of evil and envy (Surahs 7:200; 68:51; 113:5), while Hadith explicitly addresses its reality and prescribes protective measures.

In Islam, the evil eye (*al ayn*) is closely associated with envy (*hasad*), believed to cause harm or illness by directing envy toward another's blessings or good fortune. This belief is often invoked to explain unexplained sickness or disability, with many attributing such conditions to the malevolent effects of the evil eye.

To protect against the evil eye, Muslims employ various measures such as charms, amulets, and incantations. These include carrying miniature Qur'ans, using the Hand of Fatimah (*hamsa*), inscribing Qur'anic verses, or reciting specific prayers and spells. The Hand of Fatimah, symbolizing protection, is widely recognized across the Middle East and North Africa, often adorned with Qur'anic inscriptions or other protective symbols.

Incantation bowls inscribed with Arabic verses are also utilized for healing purposes, believed to absorb the healing power of the Qur'an. Practices such as burning incense with specific invocations are common rituals against the evil eye in cultures influenced by Islamic traditions.

Islamic practices such as *Dhikr*, the ritual invocation and remembrance of God, play a central role in both orthodox and folk Islam. *Dhikr* is commonly practiced among Muslims. *Dhikr* can focus on more than just the name Allah. God's attributes and ninety-nine names are frequently chanted in *dhikr* fashion. Sufis heavily rely on this practice to seek union with God. However, *dhikr* serves not only as a spiritual practice but also as a means of seeking protection against the evil eye and other spiritual threats.

Islamic beliefs and practices are far from monolithic, contrary to a naïve perception of Islam as a unified, monotheistic religion. Scholars have long debated the essence of Islam, often highlighting a dichotomy between orthodox and folk expressions of the faith. Folk Islam, predominantly practiced by rural and tribal communities, encompasses popular rituals that address everyday human concerns and seek protection against spiritual forces. It coexists alongside orthodox Islam, which is adhered to by urban scholars and those strictly following religious doctrines. However, the distinction between folk and orthodox Islam is not rigid but fluid, with mutual influences evident between the two.

The dichotomy between orthodox (high) Islam and folk (low) Islam reflects a spectrum rather than a stark division. Orthodox Islam emphasizes scholarly interpretations and adherence to canonical texts, while folk Islam includes popular beliefs and practices prevalent among less educated or rural populations. These practices often involve rituals aimed at managing daily challenges and invoking divine blessings, particularly against spiritual dangers like the evil eye.

It is important to note that this general dichotomy can be inadequate and misleading. As we will see in the life stories of young, educated Jordanian Muslim women later in this study, orthodox beliefs and practices and folk practices seamlessly flow through their lives. Paul Hiebert describes folk Islam as being concerned with daily human problems and seeking power and blessings to control the spiritual beings and forces that inhabit our world.[18] Given that this study focuses on the evil eye as perceived by Arab Muslim women, it is vital to acknowledge the significance of popular beliefs and practices in Islam, especially among women.

While certain folk practices are more pronounced in regions such as South Asia and non-Arab countries, the belief in and practices against the evil eye are prevalent across the Arab world.

18. Hiebert, "Power Encounter," 47.

Folk Islam's influence extends widely and is estimated to impact 70 percent of Muslims globally. In Lebanon, for instance, both Muslims and Christians visit shrines seeking remedies and blessings, illustrating the enduring impact of folk beliefs alongside orthodox religious practices.

In conclusion, the belief in the evil eye is deeply entrenched in Islamic culture, entwined with ancient animistic beliefs and practices. It continues to shape daily life, particularly in communities where folk Islamic traditions prevail, serving as a spiritual resource to navigate both spiritual and worldly challenges effectively.

PREVENTIVE METHODS AND CURES FOR THE EVIL EYE

The fear of the evil eye has driven ancient societies to devise numerous protective measures against its perceived harm. Across cultures and religions, various methods—amulets, words of power, and gestures—have been employed to ward off its influence and safeguard against misfortune.

Amulets, Charms, and Talismans

Amulets and talismans have been universal tools of protection throughout history, embraced by diverse cultures and faith traditions, including pagans, Christians, Jews, and others. These objects, regardless of their specific names (amulets, charms, or talismans), are believed to possess mystical powers capable of warding off curses, promoting health, and attracting prosperity. Ancient archaeological finds unearth thousands of anti–evil eye amulets, including artifacts like images, art pieces, and jewelry, underscoring the universal dread of the evil eye across civilizations.

Historically, the concept of amulets has reflected a belief that no single talisman could universally ward off all dangers. Instead, various types were worn, each believed to counteract specific threats posed by evil spirits and the evil eye. Examples include the Hand of Fatimah in Islam, which often features an eye symbol alongside Qur'anic inscriptions or protective motifs. Similarly, ancient cultures employed amulets like the phallic image with a clenched hand (*mano fica*) in Roman times, believed to symbolize potency and offer protection against malevolent gazes.

In Jewish tradition, amulets inscribed with Hebrew letters or biblical verses were commonplace, serving as potent defenses against the evil eye and other adversities. These amulets were frequently worn or placed in homes, symbolizing divine protection and spiritual strength against harm. Various apotropaic items used by Israelites are mentioned in the Bible. A form of a crescent (crescent moon) was worn by women (Isa 3:18) and kings (Judg 8:26) and was tied to the necks of camels (Judg 8:21). A *mezuzah*, a word that means a "gatepost" or a "doorpost," was a small capsule containing biblical verses from Deut 6 that was attached to the house's doorpost.

In contemporary times, blue or evil eye beads have become the most prevalent eye amulets in regions such as the Mediterranean, Middle East, and North Africa. For example, while religious practices like *Mashallah* and Islamic amulets remain significant in Turkey, the ubiquitous presence of the evil eye bead underscores its enduring significance. These beads carry deep meaning, historical resonance, and practical protective functions against the malevolent effects of envy and the evil eye.

Words of Power, Gestures, and Actions

Words of power—divine names or invocations—have been central in incantations against the evil eye across various cultures. Assyrian texts, for instance, conclude with invocations such as "By Heaven be ye exorcised! By Earth be ye exorcised!" highlighting the belief in divine authority to combat spiritual malevolence.[19] These incantations were not merely ritualistic but integrated into daily practices to safeguard individuals and households.

---

19. Thompson, *Devils and Evil Spirits*, xxii.

In Islamic tradition, written texts of the Qur'an and the muttered term *Mashallah* are prophylactics that most Muslims employ. Written charms used to avert the evil eye are prevalent in the Middle East and are more complicated. Horses and mules have a small case of brass or copper that contains passages of the Qur'an hung as a charm around their necks. The simplest form of amulet worn by Arabs is a short prayer, spell, or verse from the Qur'an or a magical name or names written on a piece of paper.

The most spoken phrase, *Mashallah*, meaning "May Allah protect you," serves as both an invocation and a compliment, doubling as a defense against envy and the evil eye. It is frequently uttered after praising someone or admiring their achievements, aiming to deflect any harmful effects of jealousy or covetousness.

Gestures also play a significant role in warding off the evil eye. The *mano fica* (fig hand) and *mano cornuta* (horned hand) gestures, found across Mediterranean cultures, are symbols of defiance and protection against malevolent gazes. These gestures, through their symbolic meanings, are believed to neutralize the harmful intentions of those casting the evil eye.

Various actions are also employed to avert the evil eye's effects. For example, spitting three times or sprinkling salt are traditional practices in some cultures, believed to dispel the influence of jealousy or envy. Similarly, giving away sweets at joyous events is seen as a gesture to share happiness and mitigate the risk of attracting the evil eye.

In conclusion, the belief in the evil eye has perpetuated diverse protective practices throughout history, manifesting in amulets, invocations, gestures, and actions aimed at safeguarding individuals and communities from spiritual harm and misfortune. These practices, rooted in ancient traditions and adapted over time, continue to resonate across cultures, demonstrating the enduring human quest for protection and well-being against unseen threats.

VARIOUS INTERPRETATIONS OF THE EVIL EYE

Understanding the evil eye is complex, as no single theory satisfactorily explains its meaning and how it works. Scholars and researchers approach this belief system from diverse perspectives, each shedding light on different facets of its cultural and social significance. Clarence Maloney aptly captures this diversity, noting, "Some think this belief as simply a superstition or classify it among the occult; but what is one person's superstition or occult idea is another person's belief or religion."[20]

Anthropological and theoretical explanations help situate the evil eye within social and cultural frameworks. Some interpret it as a cause of misfortune, prompting protective measures and folk practices to ward it off. Others link it to envy stemming from social and economic disparities.[21] Michael Herzfeld sees it as part of a moral-value system, while Peter Stephenson and Howard Stein argue it serves as a means of social control.[22] Alan Dundes interprets the belief through the lens of life versus death, framing it as a distinction between "wet'" and "dry" forces.[23]

Scholars have explored the evil eye from various disciplinary perspectives, including worldview systems, social structures, psychology, folklore, and folk religions. This book contends that understanding the evil eye offers insights into significant cultural and societal themes within specific local contexts. Here, I will examine several standard interpretations of the evil eye and evaluate their relevance to my study. It's important to note that no single interpretation fully captures the complexity of this belief system, and each contributes uniquely to our understanding.

---

20. Maloney, *Evil Eye*, v.

21. Foster, "Anatomy of Envy"; Malina, *New Testament World*; Gershman, "Economic Origins."

22. Herzfeld, "Meaning and Morality"; Stephenson, "Hutterite Belief in Evil Eye"; Stein, "Envy and Evil Eye."

23. Dundes, "Wet and Dry."

The Evil Eye as Superstition

Early modern perspectives often dismissed the evil eye as a primitive superstition prevalent among less educated or backward societies. Authors such as Jahn, Elworthy, and Westermarck collected extensive evidence on evil eye beliefs and practices, emphasizing its persistence across cultures.[24] Edward Westermarck, for instance, documented Arab tribes' rituals in Morocco but refrained from personal interpretation.

Story, reflecting on his experiences in Italy, highlighted the pervasive influence of the evil eye, particularly among the less educated.[25] However, this view contrasts with evidence from ancient Greek and Roman writings, where the belief was discussed among the educated elite, including Plutarch and Pliny.

Elworthy and Helmut Schoeck suggest that the evil eye remains a deeply ingrained superstition affecting contemporary cultures across Europe and beyond, despite Enlightenment efforts to discredit such beliefs.[26] These early scholars, rooted in Western scientific perspectives, provided descriptive accounts but often overlooked deeper cultural meanings and implications. Recent scholarship critiques this view, approaching the evil eye from multidisciplinary perspectives.

The Evil Eye as Folk Belief and Folklore

Many scholars explore the evil eye as a significant aspect of folk belief, emphasizing its role in cultural practices rather than dismissing it as mere superstition. Dundes compiled diverse scholarly contributions worldwide, highlighting its pervasive influence across Indo-European and Semitic cultures. He sees it not as an

---

24. Jahn, "Über den Aberglauben"; Elworthy, *Evil Eye*; Westermarck, *Ritual and Belief*.
25. Story, *Castle St. Angelo*, 193.
26. Elworthy, *Evil Eye*; Schoeck, "Evil Eye," 193.

outdated superstition but as a powerful cultural force shaping behavior and beliefs.[27]

Elliott's extensive research on the evil eye in ancient cultures and biblical texts reveals its integration into religious and cultural frameworks, suggesting this folk belief was discussed in educated Greek society and considered a social and moral issue more than a superstition. His research provides insight into understanding biblical communities, their ancient roots, and their surrounding cultural influence. Elliott treats the evil eye belief and its complex not as a vulgar superstition or deluded magic but as a physiological, psychological, and moral phenomenon and an instance of folk belief and folklore.[28]

Folklore, defined as the spontaneous cultural expressions among communities, plays a crucial role in perpetuating the evil eye belief across generations. Its organic nature reflects its ongoing significance in cultural identity and social practices.

The Evil Eye as an Explanation of Misfortunes and Illness

The evil eye, deeply rooted in traditional societies, serves as a potent explanation for misfortunes and illnesses alongside beliefs in spirits and supernatural forces. Studies by Clinton Bailey and Aref Abu-Rabia among Bedouins illuminate how the evil eye functions as a mechanism to interpret social problems and misfortunes, grounded in fears of envy and jealousy.[29]

Among Bedouins, who navigate uncertain and harsh desert environments, the concept of the evil eye is profoundly ingrained. Bedouins live with a constant awareness of potential encounters with this malevolent gaze, believing that many deaths and hardships are attributed to its influence rather than to direct divine intervention. Similarly, Frode F. Jacobsen's research on Beja pastoral nomads in Sudan reveals a preference for attributing sickness and

---

27. Dundes, *Evil Eye*.
28. Elliott, *Beware the Evil Eye*.
29. Bailey, "Bedouin Religious Practices"; Abu-Rabia, "Evil Eye."

misfortune to the evil eye, particularly when the causes are perceived as nonnatural or originating from the unpredictable spirit world or individuals.[30]

G. Hussein Rassool provides an Islamic perspective on the evil eye and spirit possession, viewing them as psycho-spiritual phenomena deeply integrated into diverse Muslim worldviews on mental health and illness. This contrasts sharply with Western medical perspectives, highlighting how beliefs in black magic, witchcraft, jinn, and the evil eye can be seen as causing both mental and physical health problems in Muslim communities.[31] For instance, some parents may explain their children's disabilities through the curse of the evil eye or envy.

Even in modern contexts, these beliefs persist among Middle Eastern communities, shaping perceptions of health issues despite advancements in education and modernization. The continued adherence to such beliefs among educated populations underscores the resilience of traditional cultural frameworks in interpreting and addressing adversity.

These studies collectively emphasize that the evil eye serves not only as a cultural explanation for misfortune but also as a social mechanism through which communities navigate uncertainty and assign meaning to inexplicable events. Its enduring presence underscores the complex interplay between belief systems, cultural identity, and psychological well-being in traditional and contemporary societies alike.

The Evil Eye as a Conveyor of Envy

One of the prevalent interpretations of the evil eye is to analyze how it is associated with the emotion of envy. The ancients believed the eye was an active organ and projected envy, which they believed was a dangerous emotion. It's important to distinguish envy from jealousy, though these terms are often used interchangeably today.

---

30. Jacobsen, "Interpretations of Sickness."
31. Rassool, *Evil Eye, Jinn Possession*.

Evil Eye Belief and Practice

Envy, in terms of its social dynamics, expresses displeasure at the possessions of others, the desire to acquire something possessed by another person; jealousy is fear of losing to others that which one possesses. Envy is aggressive in nature, whereas jealousy tends to be protective. Envy is not "I, too, must have what he has," but "I want him not to have what he has, because it makes me feel I am less."[32]

Scholars often analyze the evil eye through the lens of envy and the concept of limited good. George Foster, a leading figure in this approach, developed the "image of limited good" model, which suggests that in many peasant cultures, resources like friendship, love, and material possessions are perceived as finite.[33] This perception fosters behaviors such as suspicion, mistrust, envy, jealousy, and even anger towards those perceived as more fortunate. Envious behavior is particularly pronounced in societies where there's a scarcity of desirable goods and opportunities.

Foster argues that envious behavior is very apparent in deprived peasant societies, and insufficient quantity of the good things in life underlies a great deal of envy. He identifies four common responses to the threat of envy: concealment, denial, symbolic sharing, and genuine sharing. For instance, in Jordanian culture, if a guest admires an item, it's customary for the host to offer it as a gift. The guest is expected to decline out of politeness, showcasing a form of symbolic sharing.[34]

Bruce J. Malina offers insights into how the perception of limited resources shapes envy. In ancient Mediterranean societies, individuals often viewed their social standing as fixed and limited by their village's resources. Any increase in one person's fortune was perceived as a threat to others, intensifying feelings of envy.[35]

Boris Gershman argues that the evil eye belief system can promote behaviors that mitigate envy, serving as a cultural defense

---

32. Elster, "Envy in Social Life," 49.
33. Foster, "Peasant Society," 296–97.
34. Foster, "Anatomy of Envy."
35. Malina, *New Testament World*, 81–120.

mechanism. This belief is more prevalent in agropastoral societies with high inequality and low political centralization.[36]

While envy undoubtedly plays a role in the evil eye belief system, it doesn't fully explain all its complexities. This insight is crucial for ongoing research among Arab Muslim women in Jordan, exploring how social and economic factors influence their perceptions and responses to the evil eye. Understanding the concept of "limited good" in these societies sheds light on unique behaviors and cultural practices related to envy and the evil eye among Arab women.

The Evil Eye as Social Control

Some scholars view the evil eye belief system as a form of social control within communities. They interpret the evil eye not only as an explanation for misfortune but as a mechanism to enforce social norms and solidarity. For example, Herzfeld's study in a Greek village illustrates how accusations of the evil eye serve as moral sanctions, regulating behavior and reinforcing community boundaries.[37]

SUMMARY

The concept of the evil eye dates back to ancient Sumerian texts around 3,000 BC, evolving over millennia to become a pervasive belief across diverse cultures and religions. Its influence persists through rituals, amulets, and cultural practices aimed at warding off its perceived dangers. The next chapter will delve into biblical and Qur'anic perspectives on the evil eye, exploring how these texts frame and contextualize this enduring belief system within their respective cultural and historical contexts.

---

36. Gershman, "Economic Origins."
37. Herzfeld, "Meaning and Morality."

2

Biblical and Qur'anic Perspectives

HAVING ESTABLISHED A FOUNDATION in ancient beliefs about the evil eye, we now turn our attention to the depiction of the evil eye in the Scriptures of Christianity and Islam. Understanding these historical beliefs is crucial for analyzing how these Scriptures have shaped cultural behaviors over centuries.

The Bible contains explicit references to the evil eye in both the Old and New Testaments, though these references may not be immediately apparent due to translation nuances and cultural contexts. This study focuses exclusively on these explicit references within the Christian Bible while acknowledging that indirect allusions may exist in other passages. It's important to note that Jewish sources also extensively discuss the evil eye, but they are outside the scope of this paper.

Similarly, the Qur'an alludes to the evil eye in several surahs, complemented by Hadiths that report sayings of Prophet Muhammad related to this phenomenon. Comparing interpretations across these scriptures reveals both commonalities and divergences in understanding and application.

Fear of the Evil Eye

THE EVIL EYE TEXTS IN THE OLD TESTAMENT

Deuteronomy 15:9 (15:7-11)

> 7 If there be among you a poor man of one of thy brethren within any of thy gates in thy land which the LORD thy God giveth thee, thou shalt not harden thine heart, nor shut thine hand from thy poor brother: 8 But thou shalt open thine hand wide unto him, and shalt surely lend him sufficient for his need, in that which he wanteth. 9 Beware that there be not a thought in thy wicked heart, saying, The seventh year, the year of release, is at hand; and *thine eye be evil* against thy poor brother, and thou givest him nought; and he cry unto the LORD against thee, and it be sin unto thee. 10 Thou shalt surely give him, and thine heart shall not be grieved when thou givest unto him: because that for this thing the LORD thy God shall bless thee in all thy works, and in all that thou puttest thine hand unto. 11 For the poor shall never cease out of the land: therefore I command thee, saying, Thou shalt open thine hand unto thy brother, to thy poor, and to thy needy, in thy land.

This passage describes the regulations for the year of release. The Israelites are commanded to release the debts of their fellow men and treat the poor justly (15:1–11), as well as to set free fellow enslaved Israelites in the seventh year (15:12–18). A clear warning is given to guard the heart against disobeying these commands. Verses 7–11 express a concern with the evil eye in the treatment of needy fellow men (brothers).

Reference to the evil eye occurs in verse 9. The Hebrew expression *ra'a ayinka* literally means "your eye be evil." The Hebrew word *ra'a* means to be wicked, evil (ethically), to do an injury, or to do evil.[1] Nili Wazana points out that when the substantive "eye" appears together with the verb designating evil, it reflects negative characteristics associated with human interactions such as

---

1. See "7489a.raa" at https://biblehub.com/hebrew/7489a.htm.

stinginess, greed, and envy, and always refers to a person, rather than to an independent evil power.[2]

The KJV translates "thine eye be evil," but most English translations render the meaning of the words—hostile (RSV), grudge (ESV), malicious (NASB), or ill will (NIV)—rather than give a literal translation. The reference to the evil eye in this passage can be examined based on the context of the law given by Moses. When the time nears to release the debt of the poor fellow men in the community, the rich might be tempted not to do so. Their hearts might be hardened with evil thoughts or grudges.

Verses 9 and 10 link the evil eye to the heart and thoughts of a person. Thus, the evil eye in verse 9 signifies a covetous disposition, which is the opposite of generous giving in verse 10. The usage here makes it clear that Jesus's use of the good and bad eyes in the gospel has to do with attitudes of generosity or meanness. In this instance, the text refers to a hostile and malicious nature, giving begrudgingly or being miserly, stingy, and tightfisted, the opposite of giving generously with open hands. It links the motifs of wealth, the open/closed hand, with the combination "thine eye be evil."[3]

This warning against an evil eye reflects the social concern for mutual support and covenantal solidarity in a society plagued by economic disparity, conflict, suspicion of wealth, perception of limited good, and occasions of severe deprivation.[4] The description of the needy person as "neighbor" and "brother" reminds the reader of covenant and kinship solidarity. The Israelite community should have been characterized by each acting as if the others were neighbors and family. This is seen in the repeated use of the second-person singular possessive suffix "your"—one of *your* brothers, in *your* towns, open *your* hand, to *your* poor person, in *your* land (vv. 7, 11).[5] The poor and needy are not merely a social classification

---

2. Wazana, "Case of Evil Eye," 687.
3. Wazana, "Case of Evil Eye," 687.
4. Elliott, *Beware the Evil Eye*, 3:51.
5. Wright, *Deuteronomy*, 191.

but *your* community. It calls for a relational, personal, and social responsibility of generosity and care for the community.[6]

Deuteronomy 28:54, 56 (28:53–57)

> 54 So that the man that is tender among you, and very delicate, *his eye shall be evil* toward his brother, and toward the wife of his bosom, and toward the remnant of his children which he shall leave.... 56 The tender and delicate woman among you, which would not adventure to set the sole of her foot upon the ground for delicateness and tenderness, *her eye shall be evil* toward the husband of her bosom, and toward her son, and toward her daughter.

In this passage, amid vivid depictions of divine curses upon a disobedient Israel, the concept of the evil eye resurfaces. The divine curses are described in gruesome detail, including what would happen during the siege of the Babylonian invasion of 587 BC. Regarding the siege, the Scriptures foretell that a man will eat his children and not share the flesh of his children with his fellow men (brothers) or even with his wife. It is horrific how starvation would cause Israelites to act inhumanely and subject an evil eye toward their own family and fellow men. This is an extreme reference to the evil eye in the Bible.

In describing starvation and cannibalism in the siege, the evil eye is mentioned twice—in verses 54 and 56. The KJV maintains the literal wording "his/her eye shall be evil," while other translations render its sense—(be)grudge food (ESV, NIV, RSV), envy or stingy (Wycliff Bible), and hostile (NASB). As a result, modern readers are not aware of the evil eye metaphor in the Bible.

"Begrudge" can be an evil eye holding back something or an evil eye begrudgingly envying something enjoyed by another. In the present text, looking with an evil eye involves begrudgingly withholding something desperately needed by a relative for

---

6. Wright, *Deuteronomy*, 191.

survival. Holding back something that is needed links the text to Deut 15:9 and another text warning against the evil eye in Prov 23:6.

These passages serve as poignant reminders within a biblical narrative of the importance of communal responsibility and the dire consequences of failing to uphold justice and compassion. They illustrate how the concept of the evil eye is used metaphorically to critique behaviors that undermine community well-being.

Proverbs 23:6 (23:6–8)

> 6 Eat thou not the bread of *him that hath an evil eye,* neither desire thou his dainty meats: 7 For as he thinketh in his heart, so is he: Eat and drink, saith he to thee; but his heart is not with thee. 8 The morsel which thou hast eaten shalt thou vomit up, and lose thy sweet words.

This passage offers guidance on social behavior when invited to a meal. Translations vary: the KJV and ASV use "him that hath an evil eye," while others interpret it as "selfish" (NASB), "stingy" (ESV, NLT), or "begrudging" (NIV). In Israelite society, hospitality and expected social norms dictate that a host invites guests to meals. However, despite outward appearances of generosity, the host's true intentions are revealed by his "evil eye." Verses 6–7 imply that he begrudges giving, indicating a stingy nature. This warning contrasts sharply with Prov 22:9, which praises the generous man with a "bountiful eye," who shares freely with the poor. The Hebrew word *towb* in Prov 22:9, translated as "bountiful," emphasizes kindness and generosity. The connection between the eye and the heart in verse 7 mirrors Deut 15:9's emphasis on inner attitudes affecting outward actions.

Verse 8 warns that the meal provided by a stingy host may lead to unpleasant consequences: the food enjoyed may come back up in vomit, and any flattering words exchanged will be wasted. This portrayal of the evil eye highlights its association with potential harm and illness, reflecting common ancient beliefs, but it does not attribute such effects to demonic powers.

Proverbs 28:22

> He that hasteth to be rich *hath an evil eye*, and considereth not that poverty shall come upon him.

This proverb describes a person driven by a desire for wealth, characterized as having an evil eye. The KJV and NASB translate it as "he that hath an evil eye," while other translations render it as "stingy" (ESV, NIV, NET) or "greedy" (NLT). The Septuagint (LXX) translates it as "envious."

John Gill's commentary interprets the evil eye here as indicative of envy and covetousness, contrasting it with a "good" or "bountiful" eye that reflects generosity. He elucidates further, noting that the person in question envies others' wealth, begrudging anything that goes beyond his own possessions.[7] This attitude drives him to pursue wealth hastily, motivated by a desire to match or exceed others in material wealth. The proverb underscores the contrast between a covetous, envious disposition and a generous, liberal spirit.

These Old Testament references do not imply that the evil eye is a magical or evil power that causes misfortunes, nor is it an evil eye demon, as the Greeks thought. They rather convey how the eye expresses a person's heart and inner disposition, such as stinginess, greed, and begrudging, especially those who are rich and wealthy.

THE EVIL EYE TEXTS IN THE NEW TESTAMENT

References to the evil eye in the New Testament are primarily found in the teachings of Jesus, as recorded by three Gospel writers: Matthew's Sermon on the Mount (Matt 6), Luke's parallel account (Luke 11), the parable of the laborers in the vineyard (Matt 20), and a list of vices in Mark 7. This discussion will focus on Matthew's record from the Sermon on the Mount.

Apart from Jesus, the apostle Paul also references the evil eye in his Letter to the Galatians, which will be examined to understand

---

7. Gill, *Proverbs*, Prov. 28:22.

its implications among early Christians. This analysis considers the social and cultural context of the first-century Mediterranean world and the specific background of the Galatian church to grasp Paul's intended message concerning the evil eye.

Matthew 6:22–23 (Luke 11:33–36)

> 22 The light of the body is the eye: if therefore thine eye be single, thy whole body shall be full of light. 23 But *if thine eye be evil*, thy whole body shall be full of darkness. If therefore the light that is in thee be darkness, how great is that darkness!

Interpretations of this saying vary widely, particularly regarding the meanings of "good," "bad," "evil," and "eye," without achieving consensus on the exact significance. The Greek word *haplous* in verse 22 is translated as "single" (KJV), "good" (NIV), "clear" (NASB), "healthy" (NET, ESV), and "sound" (J. B. Phillips). In verse 23, *ponéros* is translated as "evil" (KJV, J. B. Phillips), "unhealthy" (NIV), and "bad" (ESV).

Many commentaries approach this passage theologically, emphasizing lessons for modern readers. For instance, some interpret a "single eye" as being focused solely on heavenly treasures, contrasting it with an "evil eye" that is envious and greedy. However, these interpretations often overlook the social and cultural context in which Jesus originally spoke these words.

In ancient times, the eye was understood as an active organ that emitted light, revealing inner attitudes and dispositions. The metaphor of the eye as the lamp of the body reflects this premodern understanding, contrasting with the modern theory of light entering the eye to enable vision. Understanding this ancient worldview is crucial for interpreting the concept of the evil eye in the Gospels.

Commentators like William Hendriksen suggest that *haplous*, meaning "single," "simple," or "uncomplicated," develops nuanced meanings elsewhere in the New Testament, such as "sincerity" (Eph 6:5), "liberality" (Rom 12:8; 2 Cor 8:2; 9:11, 13), and "generosity"

(Jas 1:5). A "good" eye reflects a generous and benevolent nature, while an "evil eye" denotes stinginess, envy, or greed.

Matthew links the eye with the heart in this saying, which is consistent with ancient beliefs that viewed the eye as expressing the emotions and intentions of the heart, particularly envy. This aligns with the Old Testament's usage of the evil eye found in Proverbs.

Jesus's teachings addressed communities familiar with the belief in the evil eye, prevalent in surrounding nations. However, it's crucial to note that biblical references do not attribute supernatural powers to the evil eye for cursing. Instead, they highlight the eye as a window into a person's moral disposition. Biblical teachings do not equate the evil eye with sorcery or magic but emphasize its connection to envy, greed, and the cultural notion of "limited good" in competitive societies.

This saying also appears in Luke's Gospel but within a different context. Since Matthew's version has been discussed here, Luke's version will not be examined again. Nevertheless, David Fiensy's insights on the background and cultural understanding of the ancient world provide additional context, interpreting Jesus's teachings through the lens of the belief in the evil eye.[8]

In conclusion, biblical references to the evil eye illuminate its role in ancient perceptions of envy and greed, contextualizing Jesus's teachings within a framework that challenges listeners to examine their inner motivations and intentions.

Matthew 20:15 (1–15)

> Is it not lawful for me to do what I will with mine own? Is *thine eye evil*, because I am good?

In Matt 20:15, Jesus uses the phrase "Is thine eye evil, because I am good?" within the context of the parable of the laborers in the vineyard (Matt 20:1–15). This parable illustrates a scenario where a vineyard owner hires workers at different times throughout the day but pays them all the same wage at the end of the day, much to

---

8. Fiensy, "Evil Eye," 88.

the dissatisfaction of those who were hired first and worked longer hours.

The phrase "is thine eye evil" in the KJV reflects Jesus addressing those who were dissatisfied with the fairness of the owner's generosity. Other translations interpret this phrase to mean "envious" (NIV), "begrudge" (ESV, RSV), or "wicked" (Wycliffe Bible). The context of the parable situates the vineyard owner as a representative of God, who demonstrates abundant grace and generosity by paying all workers equally, regardless of the hours worked. This contrasts with the attitude of the first hired workers, who exhibit an "evil eye," characterized by envy, stinginess, and discontentment with the owner's gracious actions.

The term "evil eye" here reflects an ancient belief that one's eye reveals one's inner disposition, particularly regarding envy and greed. Jesus uses this concept to highlight the contrast between God's generous nature and the human tendency towards jealousy and a scarcity mindset. By rebuking those with an evil eye, Jesus challenges his listeners to embrace generosity and rejoice in the blessings of others rather than harbor envy.

Mark 7:20–23

> 20 And he said, That which cometh out of the man, that defileth the man. 21 For from within, out of the heart of men, proceed evil thoughts, adulteries, fornications, murders, 22 thefts, covetousness, wickedness, deceit, lasciviousness, *an evil eye*, blasphemy, pride, foolishness: 23 All these evil things come from within, and defile the man.

Mark 7:22 provides another reference to the evil eye within a list of vices that originate from within a person's heart. Here, Jesus teaches that defilement comes from within a person, stemming from his thoughts and intentions rather than external sources. Within this list of vices, "an evil eye" (*ophthalmos ponéros*) is mentioned alongside other moral failings like greed, deceit, and pride. The term is translated as "envy" in modern versions (ESV, RSV, NIV, NET, J. B.

Phillips, NLT), reflecting its association with a malevolent disposition towards others' success or possessions.

In biblical and ancient Mediterranean contexts, the evil eye was understood not as a supernatural force but as a metaphor for a person's internal attitudes of envy and greed. It symbolizes a heart disposition that is resentful and covetous, lacking generosity and contentment. Unlike surrounding cultures that attributed the evil eye to a demonic entity capable of causing harm, biblical texts emphasize its human origin and moral implications.

The references to the evil eye in the Gospels underscore Jesus's teachings on internal moral integrity and the dangers of envy and greed. These passages challenge listeners to examine their hearts and cultivate attitudes of generosity, gratitude, and contentment rather than succumbing to envy or covetousness. The biblical understanding of the evil eye contrasts sharply with externalized supernatural beliefs prevalent in neighboring cultures, reinforcing its moral and ethical dimensions within everyday human conduct.

By addressing the evil eye in these contexts, Jesus teaches a transformative ethic that values generosity and celebrates the blessings of others, thus promoting communal harmony and spiritual growth among his followers.

Galatians 3:1

> O foolish Galatians, who hath *bewitched* you?

In Gal 3:1, the apostle Paul employs vivid language to confront the Galatian believers who have been swayed from the true gospel he preached. He addresses them as "O foolish Galatians, who hath bewitched you?" The term "bewitched" in the KJV comes from the Greek word *ebaskanen*, which in this context carries the implication of being enchanted, fascinated, or put under a spell.

To fully grasp the meaning of "bewitched" in this passage, it's crucial to consider the cultural and social context of the first-century Greco-Roman world. During this period, beliefs in supernatural influences such as witchcraft, spells, and the evil eye were widespread. The evil eye, known as *baskania* in Greek or *fascinatio* in Latin, referred to the harmful power believed to emanate from jealous or envious looks. This concept was deeply embedded in the cultural psyche, where people feared that envy or malevolent intentions could cause harm or misfortune to others.

Paul's use of "bewitched" taps into this cultural backdrop. By accusing the Galatians of being bewitched, Paul suggests that they have been ensnared or entranced by false teachings that have led them astray from the gospel of grace. These false teachings, likely propagated by Judaizers who emphasized adherence to the Mosaic law for salvation, undermined the Galatians' understanding of justification by faith in Christ alone.

Moreover, the accusation of being bewitched carries rhetorical weight. It not only highlights the seriousness of their spiritual deviation but also implies that they have been duped or deceived into abandoning the simplicity of faith in Christ. Paul's sharp rebuke as "foolish" underscores his dismay at their gullibility in succumbing to these false teachings.

Paul's rhetorical strategy here serves several purposes. First, it aims to jolt the Galatians into self-reflection and repentance, urging them to recognize the gravity of their spiritual error. Second, it challenges the credibility of the Judaizers who had misled them, suggesting that their teachings were not only false but also potentially malevolent in intent, akin to casting an evil eye over the young faith of the Galatian church.

Furthermore, Paul's reference to being bewitched can be seen as a counteraccusation against his opponents. While Judaizers might have questioned Paul's authority or motives (perhaps even accusing him of wielding an evil eye), Paul turns the tables by implying that it is they who have spiritually harmed the Galatians through their false teachings and legalistic demands.

In summary, Paul's use of "bewitched" in Gal 3:1 draws on contemporary cultural beliefs about the evil eye and spiritual influences. It serves as a powerful indictment of the Galatians' departure from the gospel of grace, highlighting their susceptibility to false teachings and the serious consequences of abandoning faith in Christ. This passage underscores the importance of cultural context in interpreting biblical texts and reveals Paul's skillful use of language to address theological and pastoral challenges within the early Christian community.

THE EVIL EYE TEXTS IN THE QUR'AN

Muslims refer to the basis for their belief in the evil eye in their holy books. In this section, I will examine a verse (or ayah) in Surah 68 (Al-Qalam, the pen), as well as Surahs 113 (Al-Falaq, the daybreak) and 114 (Al-Nas, mankind) that allude to the evil eye. Muslims often recite these verses to protect and cure themselves. Among many English translations of the Qur'an available, I selected some recognized as the best, including those by A. J. Arberry, Abdullah Yusuf Ali, Mohammed M. Pickthall, Muhammad Asad, and Muhammad Abdel Haleem.

Surah 68 (Al-Qalam, the pen)

وَإِن يَكَادُ ٱلَّذِينَ كَفَرُوا۟ لَيُزْلِقُونَكَ بِأَبْصَٰرِهِمْ لَمَّا سَمِعُوا۟ ٱلذِّكْرَ وَيَقُولُونَ إِنَّهُۥ لَمَجْنُونٌ

> 68:51 And the Unbelievers would almost trip thee up with their eyes when they hear the Message; and they say: "Surely he is possessed!" (Ali)

> 68:51 The unbelievers wellnigh strike thee down with their glances, when they hear the Reminder, and they say, "Surely he is a man possessed!" (Arberry)

This verse is a reminder to be cautious of those who oppose revelation. According to Islamic tradition, the Quraysh were trying to attack the Prophet through the evil eye, but this verse was revealed as a means of protection. According to one report:

Biblical and Qur'anic Perspectives

There was a man among the Arabs who used to abstain from food for two or three days and then raise part of his tent as the cattle passed by and say, "There are no grazing camels or sheep today better than these," and the cattle would not proceed far before some of them would fall dead. The disbelievers asked this man to give the evil eye to the Messenger of God, but God protected His Prophet and revealed this verse.[9]

The Prophet Muhammad is reported to have said, "Seek refuge in God, for the [evil] eye is real." He exhorted his companions: "If one of you sees something of his brother, or himself, or his wealth that he admires, then glorify God, for the [evil] eye is real."[10]

The phrase لَيُزْلِقُونَكَ بِأَبْصَـٰرِهِمْ is translated with various meanings as shown above, including "kill with their eyes" and "with their malicious looks." These translations render the explicit meaning of the evil eye. Ibn Kathīr comments that the phrase بِأَبْصَـٰرِهِم (with their eyes) means "they are jealous of you due to their hatred of you, and were it not for Allah's protection of you, defending you against them (then their evil eye would harm you)."[11] According to him, this verse proves that the evil eye's power and its affliction are real. Ali interprets it with a broader meaning that evil men's eyes look at a good man as if they would eat him up, trip him up, or disturb him from his position of stability or firmness.[12] Several Hadiths also relate to the evil eye.

> Narrated ʿAisha: The Prophet ordered me or somebody else to do Ruqya (if there was danger) from an evil eye.[13]

> From Ibn Abbas that the Prophet said,
> "The evil eye is real. If anything were to overtake the divine decree (and change it, then it would be the evil eye."

---

9. Al-Qurtubi, *Al-Jāmiʿ Li-Aḥkām Al-Qurʾān*, page number unavailable.
10. Ibn Hanbal, *Musnad Imam Ahmad bin Hanbal*, 3:447.
11. Ibn Kathīr, *Tafsir Ibn Kathir*, 10:125.
12. Ali, *Glorious Qurʾan*, 1594.
13. Al-Bukhārī, *Ṣaḥīḥ Al-Bukhārī*, 71:634.

And if you perform Ghusl (to remove the evil eye), then wash well."[14]

From Ibn Abbas that he said, "The Messenger of Allah used to invoke Allah's protection for Al-Hasan and Al-Husayn (his grandsons) by saying,
'I seek protection for you two by the perfect Words of Allah from every Shaytan, and dangerous creature, and from every eye that is evil.' Then he would say, 'Thus, did Ibrahim used to seek protection for Ishaq and Ismail (his sons).'"[15]

Surah 113 (Al-Falaq, the daybreak)

قُلْ أَعُوذُ بِرَبِّ ٱلْفَلَقِ
مِن شَرِّ مَا خَلَقَ
وَمِن شَرِّ غَاسِقٍ إِذَا وَقَبَ
وَمِن شَرِّ ٱلنَّفَّٰثَٰتِ فِى ٱلْعُقَدِ
وَمِن شَرِّ حَاسِدٍ إِذَا حَسَدَ

1 Say: I take refuge with the Lord of the Daybreak
2 from the evil of what He has created
3 from the evil of darkness when it gathers
4 from the evil of the women who blow on knots,
5 from the evil of an envier when he envies (Arberry)

Surahs 113 and 114 are said to have been revealed concerning an incident in which the Prophet fell ill due to a spell put upon him by a sorceress using black magic. The archangel Gabriel (Jebril) is said to have told Muhammad the location of a knotted string upon which the sorceress had whispered her spell and then revealed these two surahs to undo the spell.[16]

The two surahs are known as *al-Mu'awwidhatayn* (the two protectors) and are used by Muslims as an invocation against

---

14. Muslim, *Ṣaḥīḥ Muslim*, 4:1719.
15. Al-Bukhārī, *Ṣaḥīḥ Al-Bukhārī*, 55:590.
16. Nasr, *Study Quran*, 1581.

BIBLICAL AND QUR'ANIC PERSPECTIVES

many evils, including the evil eye. The virtues of these surahs are narrated in different Hadiths. It is recorded that "whenever the Messenger of Allah was suffering from an ailment, he would recite the *Mu'awwidhatayn* over himself and blow (over himself)."[17] It has been reported that "the Messenger of Allah used to seek protection against the evil eye of the Jinn and mankind. When Al-Mu'awwadhatan were revealed, he started to recite them [for protection] and stopped reciting anything else."[18]

Surah 113 teaches Muslims to seek refuge in Allah from every kind of danger, evil, and envy on the part of others. Most understand verse 2 as a reference to Satan. It may also be a general reference to all that is evil. Verse 4 is translated as "the evil of malignant witchcraft," "witches," and "the evil of the women who blow on knots."

The Arabic word ٱلنَّفَّٰثَٰتِ (*naffathat*) refers to those who engage in the practice of tying knots in a string and whispering incantations over them (a form of witchcraft performed by women) but can indicate all those who engage in black magic. They can include those who engage in magic, secret plotting, the display of false and seductive charms, or spreading false and secret rumors or slanders to frighten men or deter them from right action.[19] Though the noun is in the feminine plural, as Arberry literally translates, it is not necessarily limited to women but can be understood as a reference to human beings in general.

Verse 5 seeks refuge from the effects of envy—understanding that malignant envy seeks to destroy the happiness or the material or spiritual good enjoyed by other people.[20] One of the first sins committed on earth arose from Cain's envy of Abel. Thus, those who envy the favor bestowed upon others oppose the blessings of God.[21] It has been reported that Jibril came to the Prophet and

---

17. Muslim, *Ṣaḥīḥ Muslim*, 4:1723; see also Abu Dawud, *Sunan Abu Dawud*, 28:3893.
18. An-Nasai, *Sunan An-Nasa'i*, 50:5496.
19. Ali, *Glorious Qur'an*, 1808.
20. Ali, *Glorious Qur'an*, 1808.
21. Al-Qurṭubi, *Al-Jami' Li-Aḥkam Al-Qur'an*, page number unavailable.

said, "Are you suffering from any ailment, Muhammad?" The Prophet replied that he was. So Jibril said, "In the Name of Allah, I recite the prayer (*Ruqyah*) over you, from every illness that harms you, from the evil of every envious person and the evil eye. May Allah cure you."[22]

Surah 114 (Al-Nas, mankind)

قُلْ أَعُوذُ بِرَبِّ ٱلنَّاسِ
مَلِكِ ٱلنَّاسِ
إِلَٰهِ ٱلنَّاسِ
مِن شَرِّ ٱلْوَسْوَاسِ ٱلْخَنَّاسِ
ٱلَّذِى يُوَسْوِسُ فِى صُدُورِ ٱلنَّاسِ
مِنَ ٱلْجِنَّةِ وَٱلنَّاسِ

1 Say: I take refuge with the Lord of men
2 The King of men
3 The God of men
4 From the evil of the slinking whisperer (Shaitan)
5 Who whispers in the breasts of men
6 Of jinn and men (Arberry)

The last surah concludes the Qur'an with an appeal to trust in Allah, rather than man, as a sure protection against external and internal evil. Verses 1–3 indicate that to find true refuge from Satan, people must recognize the complete sovereignty of Allah. Thus, human beings are ordered to seek refuge from the illusion of self-sufficiency that is the root of all sin by acknowledging their complete dependence on Allah by saying, "Oh my Lord! Oh my King! Oh my God!"[23]

In verse 4, the whisperer is Satan or the devil. This verse refers to all manners of temptation. The first sin of Adam and Eve was to

---

22. Muslim, *Ṣaḥīḥ Muslim*, 26:5425.
23. Al-Razi, *Al-Tafsīr Al-Kabīr*, page number unavailable.

Biblical and Qur'anic Perspectives

listen to the whispers of Satan.²⁴ Muslims believe the devil will go to any lengths to confuse and confound believers.²⁵ He whispers when one is heedless of God, and then when one obeys and remembers God, he withdraws. Ali interprets this verse as a warning, especially against the secret whispers of evil within our own hearts. This power of evil may come from Satan, evil men, or the evil inclinations within man's own will. They secretly whisper evil and then withdraw to make their net more subtle and alluring.²⁶

Verse 6 talks about the sources of evil. It refers to what whispers into the souls of jinn and mankind, to the jinn who whisper into the souls of people, and to people who heed the advice of their own whispering soul rather than the guidance of God.²⁷ It may also be a reference to both jinn and people who whisper into souls. Whether they may be invisible jinn or human beings, it advises people to put themselves in God's protection and take Allah as their Lord, King, and God.

Muslims recite the last two surahs and Surah 112 (Al-Ikhlas, purity or sincerity) as invocations against the evil eye. Several Hadiths record the Prophet Muhammad reciting the last three surahs and the specific ways he did.

> Narrated 'Aisha: Whenever thy Prophet went to bed every night, he used to cup his hands together and blow over it after reciting Surat Al-Ikhlas, Surat Al-Falaq and Surat An-Nas, and then rub his hands over whatever parts of his body he was able to rub, starting with his head, face and front of his body. He used to do that three times.²⁸

> Narrated 'Aisha: The Prophet, during his fatal ailment used to blow (on his hands and pass them) over his body while reciting the Mu'auwidhat (Surat-an-Nas and Surat-al-Falaq). When his disease got aggravated, I used

---

24. Nasr, *Study Quran*, 1584.
25. Ibn Kathīr, *Tafsir Ibn Kathir*, 10:647.
26. Ali, *Glorious Qur'an*, 1810.
27. Nasr, *Study Quran*, 1584.
28. Abu Dawud, *Sunan Abu Dawud*, 42:5038.

to recite them for him and blow (on his hands) and let him pass his hands over his body because of its blessing.[29]

The last three surahs together are thus understood to provide protection and refuge from the evil eye.

SUMMARY

Comparing references to the evil eye in the Bible and the Qur'an highlights similarities and differences between these two Abrahamic traditions and their cultural contexts. The concept of the evil eye in the Old Testament denotes primarily a person's envious or covetous attitude, contrasting with pagan beliefs where it was seen as a supernatural force causing harm. Unlike pagan notions, the biblical portrayal does not attribute magical or demonic powers to the evil eye.

In the New Testament, Jesus and Paul address the concept of the evil eye within their Jewish and Greco-Roman milieu. Jesus speaks of a "good eye" symbolizing generosity and an "evil eye" symbolizing envy and stinginess (Matt 6:22–23). This contrasts with the pagan belief in the evil eye as a malevolent force. Similarly, Paul references the evil eye in Gal 3:1, addressing envy and its divisive effects among believers.

The Qur'an does not explicitly mention the evil eye but alludes to envy and evil influences. Surah 68:51 is cited to illustrate the reality of the evil eye, highlighting its implicit presence in Islamic belief. Surahs 113 and 114 are considered protective against all forms of evil, including the effects of envy. Muslims believe reciting these surahs serves as a safeguard, influenced by the tradition of the Prophet Muhammad using them as incantations against afflictions like the evil eye.

In conclusion, while the concept of the evil eye is acknowledged in both the Bible and the Qur'an, each tradition interprets it within its own theological framework. The Bible focuses on the moral implications of envy and generosity, while the Qur'an uses

---

29. Al-Bukhārī, *Ṣaḥīḥ Al-Bukhārī*, 71:631.

protective surahs to seek refuge from the unseen harms caused by envy and other evils. Both traditions use these teachings to encourage virtuous behavior and ward off negative influences.

3

Narratives of Young Jordanian Muslim Women

THE DATA ON THE evil eye among young Jordanian Muslim women were drawn from personal interviews. This section aims to address the research questions and explore how the evil eye influences the beliefs and practices of educated young Jordanian Muslim women.

The field data reflect a blend of orthodox Islamic teachings and folk practices. While some beliefs and practices resonate with Muslim women in other regions, the context in Jordan shapes how these young women perceive and respond to the evil eye within their conservative and traditional Islamic society.

In presenting their responses and perspectives, efforts were made to preserve their authenticity, resulting in occasional instances of language that may lack eloquence or smoothness.

YOUNG JORDANIAN MUSLIM WOMEN'S UNDERSTANDING OF THE EVIL EYE

This data analysis explores how young Jordanian Muslim women understand and perceive the evil eye, and how it influences their relationships and beliefs. The insights shared highlight the prevalence of beliefs in the evil eye among educated young Muslim women in Jordan. Out of sixty participants, all but four indicated a belief in the power of the evil eye. Among these, two expressed disbelief in its supernatural influence, viewing it as either fate or the consequence of human animosity.

First, Haneen, one of the participants who doesn't believe in the evil eye, considers it a myth perpetuated across generations:

> I don't believe it. It's a myth passed down through generations; there is no fact about its power. Islam provides this thought, but people amplify this story. The evil eye is mentioned in the Qur'an, but there may be a different definition and meaning now . . .
>
> People connect their failures with the evil eye and explain them with it, but in reality, it's a failure. They think they are victims. If someone fails, he says it's because of the evil eye. It's an excuse, not a real thing. It's not scientific, just talk between people. I think it happened by chance. There is no power in our eyes to hurt people. Maybe it's negative energy; I believe in negative and positive energy.

In her thinking, people have closed minds and uncritically believe and repeat their ancestors' stories without thinking for themselves. Although people had told her that there was an evil eye when something bad happened, she did not believe it. Instead, she reasoned that many things can happen in our life cycle, which is normal. She mentioned that the belief doesn't correlate with education levels; many educated individuals still uphold this belief without critical assessment.

In her explanation of the evil eye phenomena, she noted something insightful. She commented that there is competition and hatred among neighbors and relatives who speak against each other and accuse one another of injuring with the evil eye. Often, she reported that people want to be better than others and do not wish for good things for them. This leads them to hide things. It also means they excuse their failures by blaming them on the evil eye of their nearby relatives. These accusations happen regularly among her relatives, who are her father's family and live close to them. Even though she does not believe in the evil eye, she observed how it damages relationships.

Similarly, Farah shares a skeptical view:

> I don't believe it. It's a matter of coincidence. People will blame you instead of blaming themselves. They can't blame themselves, so they blame others. They can't explain something that happened to them, so, say, it is the evil eye. When you don't know the answer, then use religion to answer. That is a stupid thing to believe . . . It is not an evil eye. The world is chaotic, and bad things happen . . . People fail and then blame the evil eye to cover and deny their failures. When they fail *Tawjihi*,[1] it is an evil eye. . . . It is not something magical . . . [It's an] easy way to blame others for your faults and mistakes.

Clearly, Farah is firmly against the belief in the evil eye. She lamented that young people still believe in it and expressed her frustration that it affects her relationships with her family and friends. Although she remains skeptical, she noted that she must respond and compliment the way people expect. If she does not follow the norms of her society, her friends will feel unsafe with her and afraid of her evil eye since she does not invoke God. But inside, she reasons away the evil eye and does not believe any aspect of magical power is involved.

These perspectives reject the mystical aspects of the evil eye, viewing events attributed to it as coincidences or misfortunes. Their views contrast sharply with the majority of young Muslim women who firmly uphold the belief in the evil eye. Additionally, two other participants, while not believing in its power, interpret it through a lens of fate and divine decree.

This leads to the other two women, who said they do not believe in the power of the evil eye yet provide a more spiritual understanding. In their view, whatever happens to us is written by God, which they said is fate and not the evil eye.

---

1. *Tawjihi* is the secondary education certificate exam in Jordan, which is critical to admission to the university and determines the direction of a student's future.

Sara explains, "It is not the evil eye but fate and people's hatred that caused something bad. Not a certain person can strike you with an evil eye but hatred." Noor also shares a similar perspective, "People say it is the evil eye when things happen differently from their hopes, but it is the fate of God." However, she still feels uneasy when people ask lots of questions about her work and express slight envy. She demands they say *Mashallah* to prevent any bad things from happening. These participants illustrate nuanced interpretations within an Islamic worldview, acknowledging the cultural significance of the evil eye while rejecting its mystical aspects.

These four women's perspectives as unbelievers in the evil eye provide insights that confirm various theories and interpretations among scholars. First, the evil eye is used as an explanation or excuse for unexplainable misfortunes and failures. Second, the evil eye is used to cover shame, especially failures and mistakes, in an honor/shame-based culture. Third, the evil eye does not involve magical power emanating from an envious eye. Fourth, the evil eye accusation is used among relatives and neighbors who compete and compare their situations with others. Fifth and finally, the evil eye belief harms relationships.

In contrast, the majority of participants affirmed their belief in the evil eye as a tenet of Islam, referencing its mention in the Qur'an and its association with Prophet Muhammad's experiences. Their belief reflects their adherence to Islamic teachings and upbringing. Many stated, "As a Muslim, I believe in its existence."

The participants described the evil eye as something beyond scientific explanation or physical touch. For instance, a chemistry teacher at an elementary school stated, "It does not make sense. I believe in it based on my religion, not on science." She further shared that she had researched the topic on the internet and consulted religious authorities to ensure her beliefs aligned with the teachings of the Qur'an. For these women, their Muslim identity profoundly shapes their interpretation of inexplicable phenomena, including the evil eye.

In this Arab Muslim country, Islamic religion and culture are intertwined, leading many women to express how deeply ingrained the belief in the evil eye is in their lives. Their comments reflect this deep-rootedness: "We live with this." "From birth, we learned about the evil eye." "It's part of our upbringing." "The evil eye is prevalent in our country." "It's widespread across the Arab region."

These statements highlight that, like previous generations and their parents, young Muslim women today also accept the concept of the evil eye. Their higher education level does not diminish their conviction. Some women, however, noted differences from older generations who held stronger beliefs and practices related to the evil eye. They remarked, "It was more common among older people, not us." "Not all misfortunes are due to the evil eye." "In the past, people would blame sickness on the evil eye from a neighbor. But now, with new developments and civilization, perspectives have changed." Nevertheless, they continue to live with this belief, applying it to their daily lives based on their own understanding and interpretation.

In Arabic, the terms "evil eye" (*ayn*) and "envy" (*hasad*) are used interchangeably, although they are not precisely synonymous. *Hasad* refers to envy with malicious intent to cause harm. The evil eye is described as causing harm by "striking" or "injuring" through envy. Jordanian Muslim women perceive the evil eye as occurring when someone wishes for another's blessings or favors of God to be taken away and transferred to themselves. This occurs when a person sees another enjoying many blessings and wonders why they lack similar blessings. Envy prompts them to "strike" with the evil eye, desiring to replace those blessings with harm, resulting in misfortune.

Participants explained that the evil eye can manifest through verbal compliments, praise, or expressions like "I wish," "I wish I could be like you," and "Wow!" Such admiration, coupled with envy, is believed to emit a negative energy that can harm both the desired object and its possessor. They emphasized that this phenomenon is not explainable by science but is considered real nonetheless.

All participants agreed that the evil eye can occur unintentionally, adding to its fearful nature. For example, admiring something without intending harm may still inadvertently cause misfortune. They mentioned instances where a mother's loving gaze at her child could unintentionally lead to harm. Ancient texts abound with stories of such unintended harm caused by the evil eye, validating their belief.

While affirming their belief in the evil eye, some women also expressed the view that its harm reflects fate, as nothing happens without God's will. They believed that God controls everything, including the occurrences attributed to the evil eye, testing individuals' responses accordingly.

Among the participants, forty-one women shared personal experiences or suspicions of being affected by the evil eye or black magic, either personally or within their families. These experiences and the stories they've heard reinforce their belief in the evil eye as taught by the Islamic religion. Their responses underscore that young Jordanian Muslim women widely believe in the evil eye, whether through personal encounters or cultural inheritance. Later, specific examples will be presented to illustrate the areas they consider vulnerable to the evil eye.

Causes of the Evil Eye

Participants provided various theories regarding the cause of the evil eye, categorizing their responses into several key factors. These included envy, feelings of deficiency or lacking something, inner spiritual and emotional states such as a "sick" heart or mind, discontentment, weak faith or a lack of a strong relationship with God, feelings of hatred and resentment, and sometimes even love directed in harmful ways. Other reasons mentioned were negative energy, not wanting good for others, personality traits like low self-esteem, upbringing influences, selfishness, comparisons with others, economic pressures, and the influence of jinn or other spiritual entities.

Table 1. Causes of the Evil Eye

Causes/Reasons for the Evil Eye	Number of Participants (Out of 60)
Envy	31
Sense of deficiency, lacking or not having something	27
Heart is not clean, mind is sick	20
Not content or satisfied	14
Lack of faith in God, relationship with God is not strong, not reading Qur'an	14
Hatred and resentment	10
Love	9
Negative energy	9
Others: Not wanting good for others, personality, low self-esteem, upbringing, selfishness, comparisons with others, weak constellation, money issue, jinn, spirit	(unnumbered)

Participants stressed that the evil eye is not about the physical eye itself but rather a manifestation of internal conditions and spiritual disposition, particularly influenced by their identity as Muslims. Many shared that envy is sparked when they observe others' possessions and successes, particularly when they feel their own economic strain or personal deficiencies. Envy, they explained, arises internally and is expressed through the eye, sometimes accompanied by spoken words.

Envy emerged as the primary cause of the evil eye, which is evident in Arabic, where the term *hasad*, meaning envy, is often interchangeable with *ayn*, evil eye. Participants described how envy leads a person to wish for others' blessings to vanish and become their own. It involves displeasure at another's possessions and a desire to acquire what others have, whether material goods, advantages, or blessings bestowed by God.

They emphasized that envy isn't confined to the poor envying the rich; it can occur in any social direction. For instance, someone wealthy in material possessions may envy another's health or children, and vice versa. This bidirectional envy within Jordanian society warrants further research.

Young Jordanian Muslim women explained that envy often arises from comparisons and competition with peers, siblings, neighbors, and colleagues. They described a competitive environment where families vie for educational achievements and material success. The competitive spirit extends to adulthood, influencing job searches and marriage partnerships among peers. Envy and comparison, they noted, are prevalent among individuals of similar backgrounds and social statuses.

The concept of deficiency was highlighted as a significant cause of the evil eye. Participants reported that envy stems from a sense of lacking something that others possess. They described how envy can be triggered simply by observing what others have and desiring it for oneself, even for trivial items like a pen. They illustrated this with anecdotes, such as a neighbor envying a working mother's freedom, which they believed led to the mother's subsequent illness and death.

In Jordanian society, with its tribal and honor-based roots, the belief in limited resources and opportunities exacerbates envy. Economic pressures intensified by historical and current refugee crises further fuel envy among the youth. The resulting competition and comparison among peers for scarce opportunities contribute to the prevalence of the evil eye belief.

Malina's explanation of first-century ancient Mediterranean culture and the world of Jesus, especially on envy, provides insight into understanding the responses of young Jordanian Muslim women. Since the ancients were absorbed with honor and thought all things in life, including friends, love, and honor, were limited, envy naturally followed the love of honor. In these societies, any good fortune was viewed as a threat by one's rival groups. People in the Mediterranean were very watchful of those who might harm them through envy.[2] Competition and comparison among friends, peers, and relatives are all too common.

The next reason given by participants for the evil eye relates to the heart or inner disposition. Participants observed that a person's heart and mind must be pure to avoid unintentionally harming others through envy. Participants also mentioned other complex emotions that arise and cause the evil eye. One was resentment about what others have and what they do not have. Thus, we find that envy can involve resentment, another emotion triggered by comparison with someone enjoying an advantage.

Resentment is a complex emotional response that typically involves feelings of anger, bitterness, disappointment, or indignation toward someone or something perceived as having wronged or mistreated oneself. It often arises from a sense of unfairness or injustice and can be directed toward individuals, groups, or even situations. Resentment usually stems from specific incidents where a person feels they have been treated unjustly.

Most women mentioned hatred and resentment together as causes connected to the emotion of envy. They also mentioned discontentment. All these answers reflect the understanding that the evil eye manifests what is inside a person.

One of the most surprising answers regarding the cause of the evil eye concerned faith in God. They linked a lack of faith in God or weak religious practice to the susceptibility to harbor envy and inadvertently afflict others with the evil eye. They noted that a strong relationship with God, as exemplified by regular Qur'anic recitation and prayer, was seen as protective against the evil eye.

As Fatima explains,

> He thinks this person has many blessings, and God didn't give me blessings. He lacks religious practice. God distributes his provision to us. God gives one with this and another with that. He does not have much faith in God. Why don't I have things? He wishes others' blessings to be removed... There are people whose souls

2. Malina, *New Testament World*, 108–20.

are sick, whose religious practice is weak, and whose relationships with God are not good. God distributes blessings to us. But he does not think that way. He thinks God does not love him. The Lord wants to see if you have strong faith or not. I must be strong in my relationship with God.

For these respondents, someone who lacks faith in God afflicts others with the evil eye and even be stricken by it.

As Doha explained, "It is due to a lack of faith. When a person is convinced of his blessings from God, he knows he will not have something more than what is written. I have children, maybe; another doesn't. He has money, and I don't. Then, he will not envy." She added that it is because a person does not understand the Qur'an and religion. This applies to the one who possesses an evil eye and the one whom the evil eye strikes. Some participants noted that the evil eye can harm those whose faith is weak. Rajan mentioned that people who strike with the evil eye are weak and do not have a strong relationship with God. She also added that one way she protects herself from the evil eye is by trying hard to have a strong relationship with God.

For these Muslim women, striking someone with an envious evil eye is an ultimate faith issue and a reflection of a lack of faith in God, who distributes all blessings and favors according to his will. Even though various explanations for the evil eye were given, this category of responses provided particular insight into how young Muslim women in Jordan may perceive the evil eye phenomena from a religious perspective.

As many scholarly sources record, there is the belief that the evil eye can harm involuntarily without the intention to harm others. Interviewees also mentioned this theme. Some women said that the evil eye has the power to harm even their loved ones. Faten told me, "I have a niece, and she is so beautiful. I injured her without any intention, out of my love." Another two women related the same story. At a wedding, a mom saw her daughter, who was so beautiful. The mother struck her daughter with the evil eye without intending to hurt her, and the daughter became blind. Later, when the mother died, the daughter's eyesight was restored. This story was told as proof that sometimes love can strike with evil eye.

Participants also discussed the role of negative energy, influenced in part by global spiritual movements like New Age ideology, which they believed could emanate from individuals and cause harm. They cited examples where unintentional harm occurred to loved ones due to negative energy or unchecked envy.

While the influence of New Age spirituality differs from traditional Islamic teachings, it underscores how global ideas impact local beliefs about the evil eye. This complexity requires a nuanced understanding of how diverse factors intersect to shape the perception and experience of the evil eye in Jordanian society.

Undoubtedly, the evil eye belief system is complex. Although it originated in Mesopotamia, it has adapted due to various factors, including geography, sociocultural mores, economic systems, and religious teachings. It should not be explained from merely one perspective but rather needs to account for how each factor plays a role in a particular context.

In conclusion, the causes of the evil eye among young Jordanian Muslim women are multifaceted, rooted in sociocultural dynamics, economic pressures, spiritual beliefs, and personal experiences. The belief reflects broader societal norms of competition, envy, and spiritual awareness, shaped by both traditional Islamic teachings and contemporary global influences.

Effects of the Evil Eye

As previously discussed, the evil eye is believed to cause harm to animals, humans, and possessions alike. It is thought to afflict the vulnerable, beautiful, and successful, resulting in a range of detrimental effects. Interview participants provided numerous examples illustrating the potential harms attributed to the evil eye, covering various categories that were both intriguing and surprising.

Participants reported instances where objects such as phones, dresses, heels, cups, dishes, household items, tables, and even cars were believed to have broken or encountered accidents as a result of the evil eye. They also mentioned cases where the evil eye purportedly caused strife between people, marital difficulties, or obstacles in getting married.

Health-related issues associated with the evil eye included conditions like low blood pressure, headaches, sensitive eyes, pimples, fatigue, epilepsy, anorexia, thyroid problems, cancer, general sickness, blindness, mental illness, night sweats, facial burns, and even fatalities.

Participants recounted instances where the evil eye allegedly led to problems related to childbirth, such as infertility or illnesses affecting children.

Financial and economic setbacks attributed to the evil eye included difficulties such as lack of customers, unemployment, financial losses, poverty, wasted money, or spoiled food.

Event-specific troubles like weddings were also cited, where issues related to wedding dresses, cakes, or music were believed to have been affected by the evil eye.

Participants mentioned concerns about personal appearance and mental health, such as acne, weight fluctuations, laziness, lethargy, unhappiness, and depression, attributing these to the evil eye. Other miscellaneous issues included difficulties in sleep, feelings of suffocation, plant deaths, behavioral changes, and anger problems.

According to young Jordanian Muslim women, the evil eye is believed to have the potential to harm virtually anyone or anything. Since these women are young and their beauty is important to them, it was mentioned often. One student provided specific instances to illustrate her understanding of the evil eye's impact. She recounted her experience where she believed the evil eye had caused her to lose weight after she had attended a party at the age of eighteen. On another occasion, she shared how her eyes had become sensitive and teary for weeks after a comment made in her presence, attributing it to the evil eye.

Several categories stood out: car accidents, studies, and hair. Car accidents were highlighted as particularly noteworthy by about one third of respondents. They expressed a belief that the evil eye could lead to fatal car accidents, especially when individuals acquire new vehicles. Participants recounted incidents where accidents occurred shortly after purchasing a car, attributing these tragedies to envy directed towards the new vehicle or its owner. They believed that as people saw the car and expressed "wow" without mentioning *Mashallah*, it caused the evil eye and accidents that followed.

Another interesting and surprising fact for me was that many young Jordanian Muslim women reported the evil eye's damaging influence on studies or grades they received from school and universities. More than one third reported that the evil eye could affect their studies, and some said they had experienced the damage of the evil eye on them or their family members' studies and grades.

In Jordan, the most crucial exam for entering a university is called *Tawjihi*.

Having this understanding, a couple of women told stories that provided a vivid picture of how young Jordanian Muslim women found the *Tawjihi* exam exposed to the harmful evil eye. As Aysha shares:

> I was studying *Tawjihi*. I was smart and wanted to become a doctor. When I took the *Tawjihi* exam, I did not pass it because I could not see the exam questions and was sleepy. I went to see a doctor, and there was no medical reason. So, I read the Qur'an for healing. Then, I became better and could study and succeed. For three years, I struggled and finally succeeded. When I was in college, I got first place in my class. My family realized it was the evil eye.

In this story, Aysha reported her belief that the evil eye made her physically unable to pass the exam. Another participant recounted a similar story as follows:

> My sister was always top of her class. My cousin was not bright and envied my sister. Then, my sister went to the hospital and could not do well in her *Tawjihi*. It was not from any reason but an evil eye. Later, my sister went to

university. Several years later, my cousin said she envied my sister and wished my sister not to succeed.

In both narratives, respondents reported that the evil eye affected students physically and mentally, so they could not test well. These women and their families initially could not understand why they had failed this critical exam. When they could not find a cause for the problem, they turned to the only answer to which they could resort—the evil eye. For them, the evil eye explains something unexplainable, including the unexpected failure of an exam.

At the beginning of this chapter, I quoted two women who do not believe in the evil eye. Aya and Haneen's remarks provide a critical perspective on the belief I am reporting here. As Aya explained, "People fail and then blame the evil eye to cover and deny their failures. So, when they fail *Tawjihi*, it is an evil eye. It's an easy way to blame others for your faults and mistakes." Similarly, Haneen said, "If someone fails, he says it is because of the evil eye. It is an excuse." These two women's interpretation starkly contrasts with the more common belief among young Jordanian Muslim women that the evil eye harms studies, even causing students to fail exams.

There were more participants' comments regarding the evil eye's harm of studies, especially involving *Tawjihi*. A university student shared the following:

> When I finished *Tawjihi*, my face was normal, without any pimples. I passed *Tawjihi*. One night, I slept, and the next day, my face was full of pimples. My ears had them also. People said it was an evil eye. When I read the Qur'an, pus came out from my pimples.

This is similar to what was shared by another university student, Maryam. She said, "And I was exposed to [the evil eye] and struck by it. I passed *Tawjihi* and got high marks. Then people said, 'Wow, what a grade!' They were surprised and said, 'You got this grade?' Then I got sick." Finally, Lina recounted, "After *Tawjihi*, someone told me that I wish my brain could be like yours. Then I became less studious."

As mentioned, Jordanian society values high grades and university degrees, especially for women. In this culture, during a critical season of life, it is understandable how vital beauty, health, study, and university prospects are for young female students. However, it is thought that the envious evil eye of friends and neighbors does not want others' success. Having success at *Tawjihi* and celebrating it is an occasion that draws the evil eye. These university students believe the evil eye exists and that people's envious words and looks cause affliction in their lives. They said they had experienced the evil eye's damage and were afraid of it and careful.

Another woman told me about her brother's exposure to the evil eye concerning his study.

> When we were young, my younger brother was so handsome. People used to say he was handsome and would become a doctor or a professor. He had friends who were not attractive and were not good at studying. My brother was smart in his study.
>
> A woman came for a birthday dinner and saw my brother. Later, my brother got sick, and the evil eye came upon him. It came upon his face and nerves. We went to a doctor, and nothing could cure him. He told us to take my brother to a sheikh. We went to a sheikh several times, and he got better. The evil eye affects your life and stays with you when you get hit.

I could sense her pain when she revealed this story. In all these stories, there is a similar thread. Jordanian Muslim women tend to assign blame to the evil eye when there is a slump, downturn, or slack in their studies and grades, instead of resorting to practical, reasonable explanations. They might have tried to explain what happened with logic but were not satisfied or convinced by these explanations. Thus, the evil eye is real and powerful to these young Jordanian Muslim women. It answers problems they cannot explain. It is embedded in their mind, culture, society, and value system.

I felt intrigued and surprised to hear about the evil eye's harm regarding studies because I had not recalled reading any similar incident from other literature. I was unaware of this kind of harm even though I had known about the evil eye phenomenon among Muslims for a long time. These young Jordanian Muslim women and university students' stories opened my eyes to see their world and understand it better.

Another intriguing category of harm mentioned was the evil eye's damage to young women's hair. Ten women commented about their hair being damaged and exposed to the evil eye. Muslim women value long and thick hair as attractive and are proud of it even though they cover it with a *hijab*. A shopping mall employee suspected she had been exposed to an evil eye.

> I had long hair and went to a salon. There were other customers, and one person told me, "Your hair is so beautiful." After several days, my hair started to fall out. My Mom said it was an evil eye. It may be an evil eye, lack of vitamins, or stress. I put vitamin oil on my body, and my hair got better later and back to normal.

Isra, a university student, also shared a story about the evil eye and her hair.

> I used to have long hair. When I went for a haircut, a woman who cut it said, "Why are you cutting it? Your hair is so beautiful!" Then, my hair did not grow long and still stayed short. It is the evil eye. She did not say *Mashallah*; that is why. This is a real story... I read the Qur'an and put the Qur'an-recited water on it. Then it came back to normal.

Basma, another university student, shared a similar story:

> My hair was beautiful. Another girl liked and envied it, so it started to fall out. I went to a sheikh, and he read the Qur'an over me, then the evil eye left my body. It happened a lot like this. I got a headache and returned to beautiful hair.

Hearing their stories helped me to understand the value of long hair among Muslim women in a new way. Young Muslim women believe their long and beautiful hair is a target for other women's envious evil eyes.

It is a common belief that the evil eye causes illness. Several women talked about sudden disease with no apparent cause found. When they went to see a medical doctor, he could not find a cause. On some occasions, a doctor told them it was an evil eye and recommended they visit a sheikh. Others went to see a sheikh and he told them it was the evil eye.

Here is what Alia narrated regarding her and her family's sickness due to a suspected evil eye. First, she told me that she believed in the evil eye. She shared that her mom's cancer and death were due to a neighbor who envied her mother's freedom to work outside the home. Then, she added more about her and her sister's experiences.

> I don't get sick normally and walk and move a lot. I do exercise. But I was sick a lot this year. Strange. My family is well, but I got sick. My friends don't move around. I suspected a little bit; maybe it was the evil eye.
>
> My younger sister was fifteen years old. We went to attend a wedding. There was a woman, and she wanted my sister for her son. She rang us and wanted my sister. My sister became anorexic, which happened after that incident. We thought it might be the evil eye. We sent her to a sheikh, but she could not get healed. We sent her to a psychiatrist, but not cured. We sent her to a medical doctor. We tried to eat together with her. She reads the Qur'an and prays, but it has not helped... It can be a mental illness, but we suspected the evil eye.

Regarding the injuries of the evil eye, there were other stories that were very intriguing. The narratives below are from college students and help demonstrate how Muslims think and believe about the evil eye. As Isra shared,

> The name of the area in the south is witchcraft [seher]. There was an airplane flying, and a woman known as evil eyed said, "How an airplane can fly like that!" Later, the plane crashed into a house and people died. It is evil eye.

Maybe the plane had something wrong, but it is so well known that it was the evil eye.

Another student Iman, who is from a very religious family with a father who is a sheikh at a local mosque, shared this story:

> I know a famous girl on YouTube. She worked so hard. Even though she was young (nineteen years old), she bought an expensive car and then had a car accident a week later. Everyone said it was an evil eye.
>
> There was another story about an earthquake in Turkey that the TikToker told. I read it. There was a Syrian woman with six girls. She was so good at raising them and managing work at home. People used to talk and compliment her on how she was so good at raising them and taking care of everything. During the earthquake, everyone above her floor in her building was alive and fine, except for her and her daughters. Only her house fell, and they died. People said that it was the evil eye. I felt afraid of it. I used to wish I wanted to be a popular girl because I am the only girl in my family and good at cooking, etc. . . . but I don't want to be popular anymore.

This girl is very young and has been easily influenced by what other people say. She noted that she did not know a lot about the evil eye but just learned from what people told her. These stories and misfortunes are difficult to explain with logic. Muslims need some explanations, and the evil eye seems to answer.

In summary, the belief in the evil eye among young Jordanian Muslim women encompasses a broad spectrum of perceived effects, ranging from minor inconveniences to significant health issues and fatal accidents. These beliefs reflect a cultural and spiritual understanding deeply ingrained in their society, influencing their interpretations of events and their precautions against potential harm.

Fear of the Evil Eye

ISLAMIC AND ARAB CULTURAL TEACHINGS ON THE EVIL EYE

The responses to the first question on how young Jordanian Muslim women understand the evil eye provided deep insights into their thoughts on its causes and effects, as well as the associated envy. The subsequent question focused on their knowledge of Islamic and cultural teachings on the evil eye, aiming to uncover what these women know from their religion and culture, despite the blending of these categories.

Regarding Islamic or Qur'anic teachings, many participants commonly mentioned that Islam, the Qur'an, Hadith, and Prophet Muhammad acknowledge the evil eye as a real phenomenon. Some noted that the Prophet Muhammad himself was exposed to and afflicted by it. As Muslims, these young women believe in the evil eye based on their religious teachings. Islam teaches that the evil eye is real and offers various incantations to cure it. Most women refer to Surah 113, which mentions the envious evil eye. While many could not recite it from memory, some had memorized it as a cure. For these women, knowing that the evil eye is mentioned in the Qur'an and Islam is sufficient proof of its reality.

The most common knowledge shared by participants concerned *Ruqyah Sharyah* and *Mu'awwidhat*. *Ruqyah Sharyah* involves the recitation of selected Qur'anic verses over a person afflicted by the evil eye. The Qur'an teaches that a person can perform *Ruqyah* by reading the Qur'an themselves, though some Muslims prefer seeking a sheikh's help. Nowadays, many Muslims turn to YouTube for *Ruqyah* recitations. *Mu'awwidhat* refers to the last three short surahs of the Qur'an: Surahs 112, 113, and 114 used as protectors against the evil eye. The Prophet Muhammad taught his followers to recite these three times every morning and evening for protection.

Another significant concept discussed was *kitman* (كِتْمان), which means to conceal or hide secrets about oneself. The term, originating from Persian, appears in passages of the Hadith and Qur'an, such as Surah 16, which forgives those who conceal their faith under duress. Muhammad reportedly said, "Seek fulfillment for things you want to finish in *kitman*." Many respondents mentioned practicing *kitman* to avoid unwanted attention from the evil eye and envy, recommending others do the same.

In practice, young Jordanian Muslim women apply the concept of *kitman* by not sharing their plans or successes publicly. They avoid drawing attention to their intentions, accomplishments, or personal lives out of fear of the evil eye. For instance, they might downplay their children's achievements or their work successes to avoid attracting envy.

This behavior mirrors practices in other cultures where concealment is used as a strategy to avoid envy. Those who fear the envious evil eye of others and want to reduce vulnerability employ certain cultural forms such as concealment and denial. One strategy for envy avoidance is concealment. This strategy is used in social interactions not only in Jordan but also in Egypt and many other cultures, including Jewish culture.

Participants also highlighted the strong influence of the evil eye, citing a Hadith where the Prophet Muhammad said, "A great many from my nation who die after the judgment decree and providence of Allah die by the evil eye."[3] This reinforces the belief in the evil eye's power among Muslims.

A common Islamic cultural practice is uttering *Mashallah*. A ubiquitous religious phrase, *Mashallah* is used to invoke Allah's protection and ward off the evil eye. This phrase is always supposed to accompany a compliment in Arabic and, at the same time, is used as an invocation not to cause an evil eye and envy. In Arab women's minds, someone who does not say *Mashallah* is a person who possesses the evil eye. It is thought that by invoking Allah's name, a person claims or proves not to have envy or intention to cause harm. Therefore, not saying *Mashallah* when giving a compliment is seen as having evil intent.

In Jordan, the lines between religious and cultural practices are blurred, with Islamic faith deeply intertwined with cultural traditions. The first interviewee noted the enduring impact of the evil

---

3. Al-Ṭayalisi, *Musnad*, 1868.

eye. One woman remarked that the evil eye does not go away till a person dies. Another respondent commented, "We live in this; whatever happens, we say it is an evil eye, which is our culture; whatever bad things happen to us, we Arabs say it is the evil eye, and we were raised with it." It is a pervasive part of Arab culture.

Interestingly, the interviews also revealed the practice of black magic or witchcraft within Middle Eastern Islamic society. While participants did not admit to practicing witchcraft themselves, their stories indicated its prevalence in their communities. This finding suggests that folk or popular Islam, with its blend of conventional religious practices and folk traditions, is widely practiced among Jordanian Muslim women.

The present research delimits the scope of the study to evil eye beliefs and practices and does not deeply explore witchcraft or black magic, even though these folk practices exist in Jordan and deserve attention. However, I will briefly discuss the witchcraft mentioned in some participants' responses. Some participants mentioned visiting a sheikh for amulets to protect against the evil eye and black magic, despite such practices being *haram* (forbidden) in Islam. Others recounted more sinister practices involving amulets or talismans used to harm others.

Gazelle, a university student, shared her personal experience with witchcraft and evil spirit possession, illustrating the blurred lines between the evil eye and witchcraft.

> I was in a school. I used to feel things and see a black figure present. I didn't tell my family, thinking they would think it was my imagination, not real. In 2017, I was sleeping and woke up and felt a black figure beside me strangling my neck and staring at me. I dreamed it was a black ghost. I told my family that I had a nightmare. We went to a sheikh and his wife. They told me that it was witchcraft from one of my relatives. There were three jinn and spirits living in my legs. It was done by one of my married relatives, so I would not get married, and even if I married, my marriage would not be happy. I had treatment for a cure. For some time, my relatives used to make these things.

> I was at home and had a parrot. She saw something that I could not see. She was afraid of the thing and hid next to me.

Her description of being afflicted by jinn, treated by a sheikh, and using Qur'anic verses and herbal remedies as cures vividly depict how young Muslim women live under the influence of folk Islam.

She explained what she did to get a cure for witchcraft and jinn possession.

> I read Surah Al-Baqarah, Al-Ikhlas, Al-Falaq and Al-Nas. Recite the Qur'an over water, drink it, and shower with it to avoid the evil eye.
>
> Many incidents happened to me. I keep salat [daily prayers]. If I don't keep salat, jinn comes. When jinn came upon me, I could not pray. I wanted to pray, but something prevented me from it. I woke up from sleep, struggling with dreams. When I went to sheikhs, they would see things/jinn. They gave me a pill that contained ingredients of herbs. When I drank it and went to the bathroom, the evil eye/witchcraft would disappear.

When I asked about protective methods from the evil eye, she answered as follows, showing how folk Islam is a part of life, whether it be black magic or the evil eye:

> Morning and evening invocations, Ayat Al-Kursi after each salat. I read Surah Al-Baqarah, Falaq, and Kursi seven times every day. Falaq and Al-Nas and Ikhlas each three times, Surah Yunus verses 8 to 82, as much as I want. Surah Baqarah.
>
> Herbs . . . Jinn hates it. Cedar leaf. I put this into the water and take a shower.
>
> Before food, I take a pill with herbal ingredients. It is impossible for jinn to come to you.
>
> When you go to the bathroom, you must read the Qur'an.
>
> There is jinn, Shaytan, witchcraft.
>
> Don't look at yourself in a mirror. Jinn envies you and strikes you with an evil eye. Our outlook is more beautiful than jinn. When you take your clothes off, you

> must say *Bismillah* because jinn is there. Jinn lives in a bathroom. You must say *Auzbillah*.
> Call a sheikh to read the Qur'an over you to protect you. *Jinn* would go out.
> Even if the evil eye strikes us, God sees how we are patient and endure.
> Everything is written by God.
> Many girls suffer from the things I suffered.
> When I went to a sheikh, he sprinkled the Qur'an-recited water, and then jinn got lost. Jinn was losing due to black musk. Through my tongue, jinn said, "No, I don't want." It was a man's voice. As soon as he came out, jinn tried to kill the sheikh. Why? Because this jinn of love loves you and does not want to leave you.

She narrated all this in detail. It was surprising and even shocking to hear. In the conservative Islamic country of Jordan in the Middle East, the fear of the evil eye and witchcraft is real and widespread among Muslim women. What she said about jinn is what most Muslims believe and practice.

Other participants shared similar stories:

> My aunt married someone from a family. But his brother liked her. But she did not choose him but his brother. Until now, he envies them. There is a thing called witchcraft in our Arab countries. He thinks about why she did not choose me and used the evil eye and witchcraft. I don't know what you think about witchcraft, but it exists.
> Some people use black magic with jinn from otherworldly beings to hurt others. It is straightforwardly noticeable that some people change their behavior. Jinn enters someone and speaks, not himself.
> I was harmed by witchcraft, not by the evil eye. Someone comes and does witchcraft to you or your spouse. Get these things through food and stomach. Eat a pill. You put this in your yogurt, and it goes away; eat honey. Drink Qur'an-recited water, and then your stomach gets better. I went to a sheikh, and he told me it was witchcraft, not an evil eye.

These stories indicate that beliefs in the evil eye and witchcraft are not considered strange but rather a normal part of life. These practices reveal a blend of orthodox and folk Islam among young Muslim women in Jordan. They seek help and advice from religious figures, believe in jinn, are afraid of jinn, and use the Qur'an as both a spiritual guide and a powerful object for protection.

In conclusion, the research highlights the intertwined nature of orthodox and popular Islamic practices among Jordanian Muslim women. Further research could explore these beliefs and practices more deeply, revealing more about the cultural and religious landscape of the region.

EVIL EYE'S INFLUENCE ON SOCIAL RELATIONSHIPS

Young Jordanian Muslim women believe that the evil eye or envy is especially likely to occur in certain relationships, particularly those with neighbors, friends, and relatives. For instance, when someone lives nearby and frequently observes their neighbors' activities, purchases, and visitors, this knowledge can lead to comparison, envy, and ultimately, the evil eye.

They reported that this phenomenon is not limited to neighbors but also occurs among friends at university and colleagues at work. These groups share significant aspects of their lives, and differences in performance can breed envy, resulting in harm, even if unintended. Maryam, a student, mentioned that the evil eye is more prevalent at university. She recounted how compliments about her appearance, major, and other aspects of her life felt like expressions of envy. Other students noted that high grades could attract the evil eye from their peers.

According to these young women, the most notorious instances of the evil eye occur within family relationships. In Arab culture, relatives are believed to strike with the evil eye more frequently due to envy. Relatives compare, compete, and desire for their children to outperform others in the extended family. They are seen as the primary source of the evil eye. Most participants (forty-seven) indicated that close acquaintances are more likely to inflict the evil eye. However, they also acknowledged that anyone, including strangers, could cause it.

The evil eye's impact among relatives reflects certain characteristics of Jordanian society and culture. Jordan is a tribal society with strong ties and tribal laws governing relationships. Rivalry between families and tribes is deeply embedded in the culture, with familial conflicts and tribal disputes often managed through delicate diplomacy. Relationships within extended families are strong yet competitive. One young woman noted that relatives often envy and harm each other with the evil eye, which she found unfortunate. This insight was eye opening, revealing a dynamic in their relationships that might be understood only through direct interviews. This competitiveness is not unique to Jordan but has been observed in Mediterranean cultures since the early centuries.

The interviews confirmed that the evil eye and envy influence relationships among young Jordanian Muslim women. It is common to hear people refer to others in their society as "envier or envious ones" (*hasad/hasudeen*) which means "evil-eyed people or possessors of the evil eye." When asked if they knew any such individuals, some participants affirmed that they did or had heard of them. Consequently, their relationships with known evil eye possessors remain superficial.

One student mentioned a specific tribe in southern Jordan reputed to be evil eyed, though she did not believe it herself. Due to the pervasive belief in the evil eye, these women are cautious in their relationships, striving to avoid drawing attention. For example, Ayla reported becoming more private about her work after an incident where she believed the evil eye caused her harm. Participants generally agreed that they maintain formal relationships with suspected evil-eyed individuals, avoiding deeper connections.

In Jordan's relationship-oriented society, it is difficult for Muslim women to sever ties with family and neighbors. Instead, they maintain surface-level relationships with boundaries. They hide aspects of their lives, refrain from discussing everything, and become more private to protect themselves from the evil eye. For example, a student mentioned her car breaking down due to a friend's evil eye, leading her to distance herself from that friend. Another participant described feeling uncomfortable with nosy neighbors and trying to avoid them while maintaining cordial relations.

Most participants (fifty-seven out of sixty) acknowledged the evil eye's influence on relationships in Jordanian society, noting that it destroys many due to hatred and envy. Farah, who does not believe in the evil eye, expressed frustration with the constraints it imposes on social interactions. She must be careful about what she says to avoid causing fear or suspicion, even among family.

For those who do not believe in the evil eye, navigating relationships in a society that does can be challenging. Compliments must be carefully given, often accompanied by *Mashallah* to avoid being perceived as envious. As an expatriate, I have also faced challenges in building relationships and giving compliments appropriately, aware of the cultural sensitivity surrounding the evil eye.

On one occasion, I conducted two interviews with a friend and the owner of a hair salon where she works. Since they believe the evil eye can harm their business, I sensed my uneasiness in interviewing them about it at their workplace. I tried not to give any compliments or unnecessary comments since I have not mastered the skill of compliments like Arab women.

The fear of the evil eye affects young women's behavior, making them cautious and protective. Many recite incantations or invocations for protection before social gatherings. Compliments are often viewed with suspicion, not taken as genuine, affecting their heart and mind.

Interestingly, about half of the participants claimed they were not afraid of the evil eye due to their faith and regular protective practices. They believe in the evil eye as part of their Islamic teachings but rely on their faith for protection, praying and reading the Qur'an. Some stated that fearing the evil eye could make one more vulnerable to it, emphasizing trust in God's judgment and decree.

Young Jordanian Muslim women are not constantly occupied with it and do not connect every bad thing that happens to them to the evil eye. They consider themselves far more educated and modern than their mothers and grandmothers, who thought everything was due to the evil eye. What they say is true in one sense—they are more reasonable and consider other explanations of misfortunes and illness.

Despite modernization and higher education, these young women still hold a strong belief in the evil eye, similar to their mothers and grandmothers. While they may not attribute every misfortune to the evil eye, they still consider it a powerful and real phenomenon. Approximately half admitted to fearing the evil eye because of its perceived power and the problems it causes. This fear leads to cautious and shallow relationships, with many following Islamic teachings to protect themselves from the evil eye.

One critical finding from this research is that the evil eye occurs primarily within existing relationships rather than from strangers. Young Jordanian Muslim women believe that its harm is more common among relatives and friends who compete and compare. In summary, whether afraid or not, these women are cautious in their relationships and use religious methods to protect themselves from the evil eye's harm. The following section will discuss the protective methods and cures young Jordanian Muslim women use.

PROTECTION AND CURE THROUGH INCANTATION

Most young Jordanian Muslim women in this study believe that the evil eye is real, is powerful, and influences many aspects of their lives. As a result, they actively seek protective methods and cures. Above all else, the respondents emphasized their belief that the Qur'an is the surest form of protection and cure. Their confidence in the Qur'an's protective power was unwavering. They expressed this belief with statements such as "The Qur'an is the guidebook and holy," "I read the Qur'an and pray. The Qur'an is enough," and

"The Qur'an treats everything." Clearly, the Qur'an is regarded as the primary source of protection and healing.

Some women provided more specific details about how they use the Qur'an for protection. They mentioned the use of *Mu'awwidhat* and *Ruqyah Sharyah*. *Mu'awwidhat* refers to the last three short surahs of the Qur'an. These surahs are commonly recited every morning and evening as incantations to protect against the evil eye and other harms. *Ruqyah* is a legislated incantation involving the recitation of selected Qur'anic verses over a person afflicted by the evil eye. It is a popular treatment among Muslims for jinn possession, witchcraft, the evil eye, and other ailments.

In addition to these surahs, some women mentioned reading Surah 2 (Al-Baqarah, the cow) and specifically 2:225 (*Ayat Al-Kursi*, throne verse) from it. *Ayat Al-Kursi* is highly revered and often recited for protection and as a means to ward off evil.

The practice of using the Qur'an for protection and healing is deeply ingrained in their daily lives. By reciting these specific verses and surahs, young Jordanian Muslim women feel a sense of security and faith in their ability to ward off the evil eye and other negative influences. Their reliance on the Qur'an is a testament to their strong religious convictions and the cultural importance placed on these protective practices.

Table 2. Methods of Protection and Cure

Methods of Protection and Cure	Number of Participants
Qur'an (*Mu'awwidhat* & *Ruqyah Sharyah*)	54
Invocation of God (*dhikr*)	32
Mashallah	27
Kitman, do not show off, conceal	26
Qur'an-recited water, Zamzam water (drink, take a bath), sprinkle saltwater	17
Other mentioned cures: Being close to God, incense, eating dates, salt, Hadith, almsgiving, following Muhammad's commands, salat	(unnumbered)

Participants reported various experiences and routines involving *Ruqyah*. For instance, one respondent stated, "If it is the evil eye, it will go away by reading *Ruqyah*," while another shared, "I use *Ruqyah Sharyah* all the time. You never know when people will strike you with an evil eye. Usually, we turn it on before going to bed. Then we sleep well." Another detailed their daily practice: "Every day I read Surah Al-Baqarah, Al-Falaq, Al-Kursi seven times. For Falaq, Al-Nas, and Ikhlas, three times each."

Ruqyah can be performed in various ways: by oneself, through recordings (such as those on YouTube), by someone else reciting over them, or by a sheikh. The practice of listening to *Ruqyah* at home or having it performed by a sheikh highlights the communal and adaptable nature of this protective measure.

In addition to Qur'anic incantations, many young Jordanian Muslim women engage in morning and evening invocations (*dhikr*). *Dhikr* involves mentioning and remembering God's name in prayer and worship, often using phrases from the Qur'an or Hadith. This practice is not limited to specific times of day and can be performed whenever one feels the need for divine protection. For instance, Nafisa stated, "Invocations are the foundation and basis of our life," while Salma highlighted her routine: "Protection methods are morning and evening invocations, reading the Qur'an, following Prophet Muhammad's commands, and protecting himself by invocations and *Mu'awwidhat*. I do it daily, and it becomes routine for me."

Another commonly mentioned protective phrase is *Mashallah*, which means "what Allah wanted has happened." This phrase is used to ward off envy and the evil eye, particularly when complimenting someone or something. It is a cultural and religious practice deeply embedded in daily interactions. Some women noted that failing to say *Mashallah* could indicate that a person harbors envy or evil intentions. For example, one participant shared, "When a person does not say *Mashallah*, I am afraid and say prayers within me. Or I tell the person, say *Mashallah*. He is angry. But he must say *Mashallah* to protect himself and us."

The practice of *kitman*, or concealing personal matters, is another method used to protect against the evil eye. By hiding their plans and private lives, young Jordanian Muslim women avoid attracting unnecessary attention and envy.

Zaynab, who works and enjoys freedom, told me that she does not share her life with her close friends, and they do not know much about her. She thinks that few women enjoy the lifestyle and freedom she has. Therefore, she is careful with what she shares with friends about her life so as not to cause envy.

Some participants also mentioned how they exaggerate the negative aspects of the things they own rather than the benefits they enjoy to prevent the evil eye. For example, they will say all the negative things and complain about things to prevent the evil eye. When they buy a new car, they say it costs too much money for gas. The fear of the evil eye can lead beyond concealing to even telling outright lies. Sajda gave the example of a woman who was pregnant with a boy but who was afraid to tell people because of the evil eye; she lied and said the baby was a girl.

Raneem recounted an incident that occurred just before our interview.

> Just happened today. I have been engaged for half a year. Some time ago, I sat down and talked to a girl and told her I had got my wedding dress. Today, I went to the bridal shop to see my wedding dress, and the owner told me he rented it out to another girl who had a wedding on the same day. I cried. It is the evil eye. I don't know who, a specific person. Maybe a girl from many people gathered together. The Prophet said *kitman*. Maybe I asked about a wedding like what, how it happens. Maybe because of that, it happened today.

For Raneem, what happened to her wedding dress was not arbitrary. She attributed this incident to the evil eye. According to the Prophet's teaching on *kitman*, she should have been cautious and hidden about her plans instead. This experience reinforced her commitment to *kitman* as a protective measure.

Water, especially Zamzam water and Qur'an-recited water, is also used for protection and healing. Muslim women may drink or bathe in water over which Qur'anic verses have been recited, believing in its power to bring healing. Some even use water that has been in contact with the person believed to have cast the evil eye.

Some women sprinkle saltwater around the house. Apart from these methods, there are other things Muslim women do to remove the evil eye—try to be close to God, burn incense, eat dates, recite the Hadith, give alms, follow Muhammad's commands, and observe salat (daily prayers).

Despite the prevalence of these practices, the participants unanimously rejected the use of blue eye beads, a common talisman believed to protect against the evil eye. They regarded it as a superstition of the old days, unlawful (*haram*), and heresy in Islam, emphasizing that only God and the Qur'an provide true protection. Here are some answers.

> Superstition is this: people buy a new car and are afraid, and then hang a baby's old shoes under or behind the car. Accessories like the Hand of Fatimah and blue eye bead. It is *haram* [unlawful or forbidden] in Islam. Unfortunately, there are many people who use them. Putting the Qur'an on a necklace is a superstition.
>
> The blue eye bead is *haram*. People put it on a cloth. It is a superstition from a long time ago. Shirk [idolatry].[4] Shirk billah. If I use it, I do idol worship because God protects me. Some people still use it. If you think it responds to the evil eye, then it is idolatry [*shirk billah*].
>
> Who made this blue eye bead? A human.
>
> Who protects us? I must be a believer in God.

The participants' rejection of amulets to ward off the evil eye was remarkable. Amulets are easily found in many markets (though they generally target foreign tourists) and some houses in Jordan. This finding serves as a reminder not to make assumptions about a group's belief and practice based on outward phenomena

---

4. *Shirk* (*shirk billah*) means associating a partner with Allah, thus idolatry.

but rather examine a specific demographic group's underlying understandings.

Some participants mentioned calling or visiting a sheikh to seek a cure for the evil eye or witchcraft. Some described initially visiting doctors who could not find any reason for their sickness. Doctors told them to visit a sheikh or even diagnosed the ailment as caused by an evil eye. Three women were told by sheikhs that their illness was caused by the evil eye. Thus, it is not uncommon for Muslims to seek spiritual and religious persons for cures for unknown causes of illness. Nada shared this story:

> I was hit by [the evil eye]. Praise God, I came out from it by the Qur'an. I felt that my blood pressure went down. I didn't want to listen to *Ruqyah Sharyah*; I felt stressed.
> I went to a doctor, but they did not find any reason. My symptoms continued. I went to a sheikh and then a sheikha. She said, "You are struck by evil eye."

The evil eye is used as an explanation by Muslim women for puzzling situations and misfortunes. Many things happen in our lives, such as sudden illness, accidents, loss, and not getting married. These things cause shame in this honor/shame culture. They can blame only the powerful, envious evil eye upon them and continue to seek relief by following the instructions of the sheikh.

Overall, young Jordanian Muslim women employ a variety of religious and cultural practices to protect themselves from the evil eye, with a strong emphasis on Qur'anic incantation, invocations, and the teachings of Prophet Muhammad. They firmly believe that only God has the ultimate power to ward off the evil eye and provide protection.

SUMMARY

Young Jordanian Muslim women believe in the real power of the evil eye, as supported by the Hadith and alluded to in the Qur'an. They understand the evil eye as something that can cause harm through envious looks or words, either voluntarily or involuntarily.

The primary cause of the evil eye is envy, stemming from feelings of inadequacy, limited resources, an unclean heart, and weak faith in God. This belief attributes the evil eye's power to a person's inner evil condition rather than the physical eye itself.

Socially, the evil eye is perceived as a threat among friends, neighbors, and relatives, often harming those who are closely acquainted. In Jordanian culture, it is believed that competition, comparison, and envy, especially among relatives and friends, can lead to the evil eye, thus straining social relationships.

To protect themselves, young Jordanian Muslim women primarily rely on the Qur'an and the invocation of God. They practice *Ruqyah Sharyah*, an incantation involving specific surahs from the Qur'an for protection and healing. Unlike the older generation, these young women reject the use of amulets such as the blue eye bead or the Hand of Fatimah. Instead, they engage in regular morning and evening prayers and invocations, incorporating phrases like *Mashallah* and *Inshallah* into their daily conversations as both cultural and religious practices.

Despite their orthodox Islamic practices, these women also engage in folk Islamic practices, blending traditional beliefs with religious rituals. They use the Qur'an not only for spiritual guidance but also as a protective charm, reciting verses over water to harness the perceived healing power of God's words. These popular Islamic practices are common among young Muslim women for protection against the evil eye and witchcraft.

4

Missional Implications and Approaches

THE STORIES OF YOUNG Jordanian Muslim women reveal a world that may be unfamiliar or uncomfortable for many cross-cultural workers. These interviews can help open the eyes and ears of cross-cultural workers to the familiar spirit world of Muslims and their understanding of the evil eye. By gaining insights into these women's fears and felt needs, cross-cultural workers can connect more meaningfully to their hearts and spiritual lives, sharing powerful truths that address essential themes.

The dual adherence to orthodox and folk Islamic practices poses challenges for missional implications. Effective ministry among Muslims requires a deep understanding of the specific contexts and expressions of Islam in the community. Cross-cultural workers must be lifelong learners, continuously studying local Islamic practices to communicate effectively with Muslims. Given the pervasive belief in and fear of the evil eye among young Jordanian Muslim women, mission strategies should be tailored to address these beliefs and worldviews respectfully and knowledgeably.

LISTENING AND LEARNING WITH CULTURAL SENSITIVITY

No matter how much we know and have experienced working with Muslim women, we must begin with a posture of learning. Our knowledge and experience will help us understand and connect with Muslim women better. However, each Muslim woman with whom we interact is unique in her thinking, emotions, and reactions, shaped by her life circumstances. This requires active listening and empathetic learning.

Cross-cultural workers should spend time listening to the stories and experiences of Jordanian Muslim women without judgment. Listening with cultural sensitivity allows us to learn about their deep fears, beliefs, and values. Understanding their worldview, including beliefs about the evil eye and other spiritual matters, is crucial. Their stories and experiences reveal cultural dynamics that are not easily visible.

While listening to their personal stories, we need to show genuine empathy and concern for the women's fears and experiences. This builds trust and opens the door for deeper conversations, leading to trust-based long-term relationships. By honoring their trust, cross-cultural workers can deepen relationships by being sensitive and respectful. Jordanian Muslim women tend to open up and share personal stories with expatriates they have befriended, often feeling safer with cross-cultural workers than with other Arab friends.

Listening to Muslim women's stories allows cross-cultural workers to engage in conversations addressing the women's fears and spiritual and emotional needs. Each woman has life issues and fears the evil eye. Discussing topics like protection, provision, and assurance, which are universally felt needs, can lead to sharing spiritual truths. These truths should resonate with their experiences and fears and be easy to understand.

DISCOVERING TRUTH TOGETHER THROUGH CONTEXTUALIZED COMMUNICATION

Addressing their needs and sharing the truths should be a discovery process together. Sharing the truth with Jordanian Muslim women requires contextualized communication, not teaching or preaching from an expert's standpoint but using a narrative approach. Personal and biblical stories, parables, and testimonies can have more impact than direct teaching for Arab Muslim women. Truths become alive and relatable through stories and testimonies from other women, matching their lived experiences.

Young Jordanian Muslim women believe in the evil eye, and many fear it because it can afflict anything and anyone exposed to it. Their fear also includes evil spirits, jinn, and witchcraft. Most believe the Qur'an has protective and healing power over the evil eye. They express their faith in God and the Qur'an as orthodox or conservative Muslims, often using the Qur'an as a magical charm.

Guiding young Muslim women to the truth about God, as recorded in the Bible, is vital. Encountering truth can remove the fear of the evil eye from their hearts. Only powerful truth, discovered and experienced, can overcome the fear of evil. Knowing the truth of God and about God is the first step to being free from evil power. As Jesus said, "If you abide in my word, you are truly my disciples, and you will know the truth, and the truth will set you free" (John 8:31–32).

Young Muslim women are gripped by fear of the evil eye, stemming from their belief in lies and a deep sense of deficiency. They believe their neighbors and friends envy and want to harm them. Envy is easily produced in this social and cultural context. Exposing lies that produce fear must be done before embracing the truth. Muslim women must hear the living truth against the lies repeated from their culture, belief system, worldview, and relationships.

Muslim women can recite familiar religious scripts about who God is and his characteristics, but they must be awakened to the truth revealed in the Bible. The Holy Bible is the best place to help them discover the truth about God. The process starts with the written truth of the word of God, followed by sharing experiences and testimonies of cross-cultural workers to solidify the truth they have learned.

Rather than straightforwardly teaching or preaching the point, it can be effective and powerful to invite Muslim women into the safe atmosphere of a discussion group where they are led to discover the core message. A discovery Bible study (DBS) method works well with Arab Muslim women, allowing them to interact with stories, apply truths to their lives, and share what they have learned with others.

God Is Almighty

Cross-cultural workers must confidently declare that God is almighty. Muslims often declare "God is greater/greatest" (*Allahu Akbar,* اللهُ أَكْبَرُ). This shared truth in Islam and Christianity must be taught with conviction in relation to the evil eye. God is powerful over evil spirits, jinn, the evil eye, and black magic. For example:

- For the LORD your God is God of gods and Lord of lords, the great, the mighty, and the awesome God, who is not partial and takes no bribe. (Deut 10:17)
- He who dwells in the shelter of the Most High will abide in the shadow of the Almighty. I will say to the LORD "My refuge and my fortress, my God, in whom I trust." (Ps 91:1–2)

Teaching about God's power should include presenting Jesus Christ, who has authority over all things, including over nature and evil spirits. Muslim women are aware of and believe in the spirit world and the works of Satan and jinn. They further believe the spirit world is connected to worldly matters and seek power to defeat the spiritual powers that afflict them. Therefore, the ministry of Jesus, as recorded in the Gospel of Mark, can help address their fear and desire for power and present him as a mighty God

(Mark 1:21–28, Jesus heals a man with an unclean spirit; 5:1–20, Jesus heals a man with a demon).

Another powerful truth from the New Testament can be found in 1 John 4:4 ("he who is in you is greater than he who is in the world"). This is a promise given to believers in Christ. A cross-cultural worker can present this to Muslim women along with her testimony as a promise that they can have too.

God Is Generous

Muslims and Christians alike often say, *Allah Kareem*, which means God is generous. Oftentimes, I have experienced women using this phrase out of habit. This shared truth must be taught, emphasizing God's generosity in providing and blessing even in times of need. The challenging economic situation in Jordan makes this particularly relevant. Contentment comes from believing in God's goodness, generosity, and provision, which combats envy and promotes generous hearts. It does not mean the woman does not lack anything. It means she affirms that God is the ultimate provider out of his generosity and distributes his blessings to all according to his goodwill. Having faith in God's generous provision gives us the power to say no to envy and greed.

- Every good gift and every perfect gift is from above. (Jas 1:17a)
- Whoever is generous to the poor lends to the LORD, and he will repay him for his deed. (Prov 19:17)

Studying the parable of the laborers in the vineyard (Matt 20:1–15) can help Muslim women understand God's generosity and renounce envy. God, depicted as the owner of the vineyard, provides work and generous wages. God's goodness, exceedingly generous character, and grace are contrasted with the evil eye of those first hired, who are marked by their stinginess toward others. The vineyard owner demonstrates his goodness and honor by showing generosity.

Young Muslim women can find out how Jesus used the concept of the evil eye and challenged hearers to reflect cultural values of honor and practice a life of generosity. The cross-cultural worker's role is to encourage and facilitate Muslim women to apply the discovered truth and teaching of Jesus to their personal lives and relationships.

God Protects

Teaching that God Almighty protects us from the enemy and evil forces is crucial. Psalm 121 can be used as a genuine prayer and proclamation of trust in God's protection. As he reigns over our lives, we can depend on his protection from the evil one's harm and attacks. Furthermore, he is the Father in heaven who loves and protects his people and children. This personal relationship with the living God, who is a strong shield and fortress and protects us, must be presented to young Muslim women.

> The LORD is your keeper; the LORD is your shade on your right hand.
> The sun shall not strike you by day, nor the moon by night.
> The LORD will keep you from all evil; he will keep your life.
> The LORD will keep your going out and your coming in from this time forth and forevermore. (Ps 121:5–8)

The interview data revealed that most young Jordanian Muslim women believe the Qur'an protects against the evil eye. Many Muslim women read and memorize certain portions of the Qur'an to use in protective rituals. It appears they lean on God and his word; however, in turning to the Qur'an, most Muslim women use it as a power object and charm rather than turning to God and his word as an ultimate protection for living relationships. The Qur'an is a more robust and legitimate tool in their religious practice. In this regard, cross-cultural workers should not be naïve but be aware of Muslim women's worldviews and folk practices. Cross-cultural workers must help Muslim women see the difference between quoting Qur'anic texts as incantation and trusting God himself.

God Heals

Many Muslim women believe the evil eye causes sudden sickness and death. Scriptures such as Ps 41:3 ("the Lord sustains him on his sickbed") and Ps 147:3 ("he heals the brokenhearted and binds up their wounds") highlight God's healing power. Studying the healing miracles of Jesus in the Gospel of Mark can draw Muslim women towards Christ's saving grace since healing is a felt need of many Muslim women and families, especially in the case of the evil eye. Praying in the name of Jesus and sharing testimonies of healing can encourage them to seek and experience God's healing.

The Gospel of Mark narrates many healing miracles of Jesus. It is filled with physical and spiritual healings of Christ that demonstrate his deity. For example, Jesus heals a man with an unclean spirit (1:21–28), a paralytic man who was brought by his four friends (2:1–12), a man with a withered hand (3:1–5), a man with many demons (5:1–20), a woman who had a discharge of blood (5:21–34), Jairus's daughter (5:35–43), a blind man (8:22–26), a boy with an unclean spirit (9:14–29), and a blind beggar Bartimaeus (10:46–52).

Cross-cultural workers need to speak the biblical truth with confidence and conviction as they invite Muslim women to study about the God who heals and frees them and to pray in the powerful name of Jesus. These are the first steps to encountering the truth. When young Muslim women hear the truth, which is the experienced truth in cross-cultural workers' lives, they will have a desire to experience and be free from the fear of the evil eye.

DISCOVERING TRUTH AGAINST FEAR

The influence of the evil eye is pervasive, particularly in the fear it instills in women's hearts and relationships. Fear can control minds and perceptions, blurring reality and creating exaggerated scenarios. Many Muslim women fear evil spirits, jinn, black magic, curses, and the evil eye. This fear, a stronghold in their lives, encompasses fears of illness, accidents, harm, curses, loss, shame, and failure. They believe harm and illness caused by the evil eye and black magic practitioners can affect anyone. Consequently, fear of the evil eye and envy distances neighbors and colleagues, further damaging relationships. Satan exploits this fear to bind people and deceive them into seeking and relying on demonic power.

Across cultures, three worldviews influence people, rooted in the consequences of sin described in Gen 3. These worldviews are guilt/righteousness, power/fear, and honor/shame. Jordanian culture primarily operates from an honor/shame worldview, with a strong element of power/fear due to Islam's animistic roots. Cross-cultural workers should tailor their message to the specific worldview of their audience, often starting where people are at.

Half of the interview participants reported fearing the evil eye. Young Muslim women are particularly concerned about falling sick due to the evil eye. This fear affects their daily lives as the spirit world is invisible and beyond human control. Commonly, Muslims wear charms and amulets for protection. However, the data collection revealed that young, educated Jordanian Muslim women do not believe in or wear amulets against the evil eye. Instead, they view the Qur'an as their ultimate protection, although there are levels of bibliolatry and magical use of the book. Understanding the specific context and group of people is crucial in ministry.

Cross-cultural workers can help Muslim women deal with their fear by studying Bible passages and teaching them about Christ's power over the evil eye and evil spirits. The Gospel of Mark vividly records several incidents of Jesus casting out demons and unclean spirits, demonstrating his power over the spirit world. The first-century Mediterranean world of Jesus is closer to the world of popular Islam than the world in which many of us live today.[1]

---

1. Musk, *Unseen Face of Islam*.

Missional Implications and Approaches

A powerful Scripture addressing Muslim women's fear of the evil eye and spiritual forces is 1 John 3:8: "The reason the Son of God appeared was to destroy the works of the devil." Thus, the Christian message to ordinary Muslim women should include that Jesus was sent by God to forgive our sins and to destroy the works of the devil. This aspect of Jesus's ministry meets their felt need.

Presenting the message of Christ will require a change in the worldview of young Muslim women. However, it's important to respond to their felt needs with a message that touches their soul and invites them to experience the power of God. As Vivian Stacey states, unbelievers need a release from bondage, and the declaration of Christ as liberator is generally more meaningful to Muslims than the promise of forgiveness of sins.[2] Early Christian confessions celebrated Christ's victory over demons, powers, and authorities.[3]

Another Scripture with impact, 1 John 4:4, which I mentioned at the beginning of this chapter, is good news for Muslim women seeking power and peace. Cross-cultural workers can witness to Muslim women through the power of God working in them. Sharing their daily walk with God and how he guides them, as promised in Ps 32:8 ("I will instruct you and teach you in the way you should go; I will counsel you with my eye upon you") reassures Muslim women that God watches over them, and they need not fear being harmed by others' envy.

DISCOVERING THE TRUTH OF *BARAKA* AND GENEROSITY

Baraka (blessing) is ultimately from God, while envy (*hasad*) is its opposing force. To effectively address the fear of the evil eye, it's essential to examine envy, its primary cause, as discussed in the Bible. This examination can provide cross-cultural workers with

---

2. Stacey, "Power Encounters."
3. Cullman, *Earliest Christian Confessions*, 24.

alternative responses and messages for Muslim women, focusing on themes of blessing and generosity, especially towards the poor.

Understanding Envy in the Bible

In the Old Testament, envy is clearly manifested in several instances. For example, Isaac's wealth caused the Philistines to envy him (Gen 26:14). Rachel envied her sister because she was childless (Gen 30:1). King Saul envied David's success and honor (1 Sam 18:9). These instances show how envy arises from perceived threats due to others' wealth, recognition, or blessings, leading to broken relationships and rivalry.

In the New Testament, envy (*phthonos*) is described as a form of evil. Pilate recognized that the Jews delivered Jesus to be crucified out of envy (Matt 27:18). Envy is listed among the evils present among early believers (Rom 1:29; Gal 5:21, 26; Phil 1:15; 1 Pet 2:1). The apostles Paul and Peter warned believers to put away envy and other evils. Paul strongly warned that those who envy will not inherit the kingdom of God (Gal 5:21). Envy, similar to the concept of the evil eye, causes social and relational discord.

Contrasting Baraka in Islam

In folk Islam, *baraka* is viewed as a mystical power, a blessing from God, believed to be transmitted through certain people, places, and objects. Muslims seek *baraka* through various means, such as visiting holy sites or touching sacred objects. Envy arises when others are perceived to possess more *baraka*, more of God's favor and benefits, which leads to a sense of deficiency and a heightened desire for blessings. As a result, they do not want blessings and good things in other people's lives but rather God's blessings to be their own. Unfortunately, many folk Islamic practices are aimed at manipulating God for *baraka*. This is especially true for Muslim women, who often feel vulnerable and seek husbands and children to bring them honor, leading them to seek powerful objects or persons for blessings.

Biblical Perspective on Blessings

The Bible teaches that God is the ultimate source of blessings and favor, which are rooted in a love relationship with him rather than mere power. God blesses individuals to be a blessing to others. This concept is central in both the Old and New Testaments. In the Hebrew Bible, the root word *brk/beraka* (bless/blessing) is mentioned 369 times, highlighting its importance.

The sheer number of references demonstrates how central the theme of blessing is to God's heart. God revealed himself from the beginning as the one who blesses out of close loving relationship. That is his nature. As God blessed, the patriarchs also blessed the next generations. Blessing in the Old Testament is often offered as a form of prayer for a person. All these examples teach us to bless others by trusting God's goodness and generosity instead of envying them.

Cross-cultural workers must first apply this message of God as the source of all blessings in their own lives before sharing it with Muslim women. God gives to each one according to his riches and perfect will so that that person can bless others with the various blessings she has received. Blessings come in various forms, not just material, and include talents and abilities to help others. God's blessings are meant to enrich communities and relationships, contrasting with the envy-driven desire for *baraka* in folk Islam.

According to the Bible, *baraka* can be gained neither by envying and wishing others harm nor by touching something holy. It is critical for cross-cultural workers to be aware that *baraka* in Islam means power rather than blessing. God-bestowed gifts and grace instead come through seeing the value of ordinary Muslim women and friends by interacting with them. As Muslim women experience blessings and strength through friendships with cross-cultural workers, they can learn how to bless and empower others who fear the envious evil eye. They can become women of blessing.

Generosity as an Antidote to Envy

Generosity counters the negative spirit of envy. Cross-cultural workers should guide Muslim women to recognize God's generosity and reflect it in their own lives. This involves acknowledging that every good and perfect gift comes from God (Jas 1:17). Stories like Jesus feeding the five thousand illustrate God's abundant provision and the joy of participating in his generosity. Notably, Jesus over-catered; after people were satisfied, there were twelve baskets of leftovers. In Jordanian culture, bread is seen as a divine gift, and it is treated with respect. This cultural value aligns with biblical teachings on God's provision.

Cross-cultural workers should begin by demonstrating a spirit of generosity and a lifestyle of sharing. By offering baked cookies and cakes with genuine warmth and kindness, they can bring joy and make young Muslim women feel truly loved and valued. This simple act of sharing can help foster a sense of community and connection. Additionally, cross-cultural workers can emphasize that God's blessings are found in relationships and community, not just in material possessions. This perspective can help Muslim women appreciate the joy of sharing and the richness of being part of a supportive and loving community.

Embracing Generosity and Overcoming Envy

Muslim women can be empowered to counteract envy with generosity, reflecting God's character. In Jordanian culture, generosity and hospitality are vital traits that have historically been essential for survival in harsh environments. By embracing and extending these values, young Muslim women can become agents of change, opposing the envious evil eye and fostering a culture of blessing and generosity.

Cross-cultural workers can challenge the worldview of limited good to bring about change in Muslim women's lives. The belief in limited good fosters envy and a sense of deficiency, blinding them to the gifts and benefits they have. Cross-cultural workers need to challenge this worldview with biblical truths about God's abundant blessings. This involves encouraging Muslim women to recognize and appreciate the diverse gifts and opportunities God provides.

In summary, addressing the fear of the evil eye involves teaching Muslim women about God's ultimate authority over blessings and encouraging a generous spirit to overcome envy. Through understanding biblical truths and applying them in their lives, Muslim women can experience freedom from envy and become channels of God's blessings to others.

PRACTICING AND EXPERIENCING TRUTH TOGETHER

To address the worldview of young Jordanian Muslim women, cross-cultural workers need to boldly and lovingly challenge hearers to begin dealing with envy and fear. In the context of genuine friendship, cross-cultural workers and Muslim women can encourage one another as they speak honestly about biblical teaching, ask questions, and pray for one another.

After the initial step of discovering the truth of God's nature together, cross-cultural workers can move toward practical application. Muslim women prefer dynamic and experience-oriented learning. To help them experience biblical truth, it is recommended to encourage interaction, application, and growth within a community context. They learn and grow better through regular interaction.

To encourage lasting change in their worldview, it is essential to present practical actions they can apply and grow into instead of mere head knowledge. Muslim women need examples and vivid stories and images to visualize, learn, practice, and experience. This way, they can grow and change as they experience the power of generosity and blessing to break the power of envy and greed. Creating a community of practice where inspiring and positive stories are shared can be effective in fostering this change.

Cultivating a community of practice can provide a supportive environment for Muslim women to freely share their thoughts and difficulties in dealing with envy in their hearts or the envious eyes of others. They need to experience genuine support and love instead of judgment and shaming from other women.

In these small social gatherings or practice groups, there is intention, purpose, and learning. They can explore God as revealed in the Bible—his protection, watchfulness, and abundant blessings—in a safe and loving environment. Discussions can include honest dialogues about the evil eye, struggles with a sinful heart attitude, learning to genuinely give and receive compliments without fearing harm from the evil eye, and finding ways to help, bless, and strengthen one another. Through this community, young Muslim women can develop a generous, unenvious outlook.

Cross-cultural facilitators are crucial in encouraging Muslim women to live honorably before God and others, emphasizing that a generous life brings honor and glory. They can model bold prayer in Jesus's name against evil powers and invite Muslim women to experience freedom in Christ together, cultivating a habit of bold prayer against envy and fear.

Last, each meeting should include sharing how they've applied these truths in practical ways. This moves beyond discussion to action, developing communities of practice that act with opposite spirit against envy. For instance, women can bring homemade sweets to share or practice generous acts with others, shifting their perspective from scarcity to abundance and weakening the influence of envy and the evil eye.

PROPOSED BIBLE STUDY

The following proposed Bible study and discussion questions serve as sample topics for a community of practice aimed at fostering growth among Muslim women. These sessions start with four thematic explorations before delving into the topic of the evil eye and related details. I recommend beginning with these passages to lift participants' gaze to God, who ministers to their hearts.

Once these themes are explored together, cross-cultural workers can choose to study the biblical truths outlined at the beginning of this chapter in a similar manner. Alternatively, they may opt to first delve into the foundational truths about God as presented in the Bible before exploring these four themes. The primary goal is to facilitate a supportive environment where Muslim women can discuss and experience transformation in their worldviews and relationships. Needless to say, such gatherings should embody generous and even lavish hospitality that pleasantly surprises the women involved.

A proposed four-part Bible study follows.

SESSION 1. THE GOD WHO SEES ME (GEN 16)

> 7 *The angel of the* LORD *found her by a spring of water in the wilderness, the spring on the way to Shur.* 8 *And he said, "Hagar, servant of Sarai, where have you come from and where are you going?" She said, "I am fleeing from my mistress Sarai." . . .* 13 *So she called the name of the* LORD *who spoke to her, "You are a God of seeing," for she said, "Truly here I have seen him who looks after me."*

Discussion Questions:

1. What did you learn about God from this passage?
2. Did you notice something new or surprising in this story?
3. Can you describe a time when you felt forgotten, ignored, or invisible?
4. How do you feel about the idea of "God sees me"?
5. Think of a recent moment or incident that reminded you that God sees you.[4] What happened?

---

4. Maltby with Buchanan, *God Who Sees You*, has a similar study on this passage. I got ideas on the questions from her book. However, my study's focus is catered to Muslim women.

Fear of the Evil Eye

Message:

In the story of Hagar, we see that God sees us in our times of need. Whether it's our physical needs like food, finances, or even emotional needs, God is aware and caring. Sometimes, we may feel overlooked or that our needs go unnoticed, but Hagar's story reminds us that God is the God who sees and looks after us. Moreover, God sees the goodness and value within us, even when we struggle to see it ourselves. He has uniquely created each of us with gifts and purpose, and he sees our worth and desires to help others.

Application:

Who in your life could benefit from hearing this message?

Prayer:

Let's pray together: "Lord, help us lift our eyes to see you, knowing that you are the God who sees us and cares for us in every circumstance."

SESSION 2. HE LEADS WITH HIS EYES (PS 32:8)

> *I will instruct you and teach you in the way you should go;*
> *I will counsel you with my eye upon you.*

Discussion Questions:

1. What did you learn about God from this verse?
2. What do you think it means "I will counsel you with my eye upon you"?
3. On which occasions would you want to have someone watch over and guide you?

Message:

God leads us in our journey through life on earth. Think back to times when you were in a new place or traveling. You likely felt nervous and unsure about what to do or where to go. In those moments, you probably wished someone was with you to watch over and guide you. Similarly, when young children are learning something new, like doing homework or exploring outside, they need someone watching over them to offer guidance and ensure they stay safe.

God watches over us with his eye on us. He provides wisdom and guidance as he watches. His gaze isn't meant for judgment or harm but to help, bless, and direct us in our decisions, work, and relationships. Knowing that God attentively watches over us brings us safety, protection, and assurance that we are never alone.

Application:

Who in your life could benefit from hearing this message?

Prayer:

Let's pray together: "Lord, help us to know and trust that you watch over us with your eye upon us. May we find peace and security knowing that we do not need to fear harm in your care."

SESSION 3. HIS GOODNESS WILL FOLLOW ME (PS 23)

> 1 *The LORD is my shepherd; I shall not want.*
> 2 *He makes me lie down in green pastures.*
> *He leads me beside still waters.*
> 3 *He restores my soul.*
> *He leads me in paths of righteousness for his name's sake.*

4 *Even though I walk through the valley of the shadow of death,*
I will fear no evil, for you are with me;
your rod and your staff, they comfort me.
5 *You prepare a table before me*
in the presence of my enemies;
you anoint my head with oil; my cup overflows.
6 *Surely goodness and mercy shall follow me*
all the days of my life,
and I shall dwell in the house of the LORD *forever.*

Discussion Questions:

1. What did you learn about God from this psalm?
2. What words or phrases stood out to you?
3. How do you perceive your life in terms of resources and blessings—do you feel lacking or content?
4. What influences these feelings?
5. How can you express feelings of contentment and trust in God, similar to King David's expressions in verses 1 and 6?

Message:

In Ps 23, King David reveals God as his shepherd who provides, guides, and protects him. The imagery of green pastures and still waters conveys God's provision and peace. David acknowledges that even in challenging times, God's presence brings comfort and assurance. He confidently declares that goodness and mercy will accompany him all his days because God is faithful and good.

It's easy to focus on what we lack compared to others rather than appreciating the blessings we have from God. This psalm encourages us to find contentment by recognizing God as our good shepherd who abundantly provides and cares for us. His goodness is constant and never ending, following us throughout our lives.

MISSIONAL IMPLICATIONS AND APPROACHES

Application:

Who in your life would benefit from hearing this message?

Prayer:

Let us pray together: "Lord God, we thank you for your goodness and the abundant blessings in our lives. Help us to see your grace and to be grateful for all that you provide."

SESSION 4. A GOOD EYE (PROV 22:9)

> *Whoever has a bountiful eye will be blessed,*
> *for he shares his bread with the poor.*

Discussion Questions:

1. What do you think a "bountiful/generous eye" or "good eye" means?
2. What would be the opposite of having a "bountiful/generous eye"?
3. How do you personally relate to this verse? Do you consider yourself to have a generous eye?

Message:

In Prov 22:9, having a "good eye" signifies generosity and a willingness to share blessings with others, especially those in need. This contrasts with an "evil eye," which is characterized by envy and a desire to withhold or take away from others.

A person with a generous eye does not hoard or give grudgingly but freely shares God's blessings with joy. This generosity stems from a heart that reflects God's own generosity towards us. The contrast between a good eye and an evil eye is stark: while the evil eye is envious and dark, the good eye finds joy in sharing God's blessings with family and neighbors because of experiencing God's own generosity.

Application:

Who in your life could benefit from hearing this message about generosity?

Prayer:

Let us pray together: "God, we thank you for your boundless generosity towards us. Help us to cultivate hearts that bless others with a good and generous eye, reflecting your own generous nature."

SUMMARY

Muslim women often seek divine blessing and protection against the evil eye, turning to recitations from the Qur'an for solace. Cross-cultural workers can respond by presenting biblical truths about God. It's crucial to highlight God's sovereignty over evil, including spirits and black magic, and to emphasize his goodness and provision in times of hardship. Encountering these truths can alleviate fears and inspire trust in God's protection.

Many Muslim women also seek physical and emotional healing, often attributing ailments to the evil eye. Cross-cultural workers can guide them towards narratives in the Gospels where Christ's healing miracles and prayers offer hope. These stories demonstrate Christ's power over darkness, resonating with those influenced by occult practices.

In addressing the fear and envy often associated with the evil eye, cross-cultural workers can emphasize Christ's authority over spiritual forces. Creating supportive communities where Muslim women can discuss and reflect on these teachings can also foster a positive shift in their worldview, encouraging gratitude and generosity. By presenting God as the ultimate source of blessing and grace, cross-cultural workers can help Muslim women find peace and security beyond fear.

5

Conclusion

THE BELIEF IN THE evil eye holds significant sway among various cultures, particularly among Muslims, who practice protective rituals due to their strong convictions about its harmful effects. Despite numerous theories, research on the beliefs of young Muslim women remains scarce, prompting the launch of this study focusing on young Jordanian Muslim women.

The research aimed to delve into the women's beliefs and perceptions regarding the evil eye and how these influence their lives and relationships. It reveals that despite their higher education, these young women uphold traditional beliefs inherited from their conservative Muslim upbringing. Their educational attainment has not diminished their deep-seated fear of the evil eye, which they perceive as a threat mainly from close relatives, friends, and neighbors with whom they compete and compare. This fear often hinders them from forming close relationships and keeping interactions formal and superficial.

Participants reported that the evil eye is caused by envy, an unclean heart, discontentment, lack of faith in God, and a perceived sense of limited good. Many young Jordanian Muslim women feel lacking in comparison to others, leading to envy and resentment towards those perceived as having more. This focus on

CONCLUSION

perceived deficiencies blinds them to their own blessings and gifts bestowed by God.

To safeguard against the evil eye, these women rely on recitations and incantations from the Qur'an, viewing it as a protective talisman while eschewing what they consider heretical practices involving amulets. However, alongside orthodox Islamic practices, the majority of young Jordanian Muslim women are engaged in folk beliefs and practices and even witchcraft.

In response, a contextualized missiological approach is recommended. Cross-cultural workers should present biblical truths emphasizing God's power to protect and his desire to bless abundantly, encouraging Muslim women towards contentment and godly generosity within their communities. This approach aims to open their eyes to the truth of their own blessings, leading to contentment and enabling them to live generously as reflections of God's character.

While Arab culture inherently values generosity, presenting biblical principles can further encourage Muslim women to embrace generosity as integral to their identity rather than succumbing to envy. This approach aligns with their spiritual heritage, fostering grace, contentment, and generosity among young Muslim women.

The effective process of discovering and experiencing the truth of God can be done through a community of practice. Inside this small community, Muslim women can ask honest questions, share insights, and encourage each other to bless and compliment genuinely and experience power against evil through bold prayer in Christ's name.

INVITATION FOR ONGOING CONVERSATION

The strategies and approaches proposed for young Jordanian Muslim women regarding the evil eye belief are adaptable to broader Muslim contexts. As I reflect on how to address these beliefs and minister to Muslim women based on their experiences, I invite other cross-cultural workers to join this process with patience and contribute their unique perspectives. Rather than remaining on the surface, I encourage scholar-practitioners working among Muslim women to test and adjust these approaches across diverse Muslim communities. This ongoing dialogue and sharing of insights will enhance the effectiveness of mission work, fostering a collaborative and dynamic approach to ministry.

A FINAL THOUGHT

If a Jordanian woman compliments another by saying, "Your blouse looks good on you!" the other woman can respond with "Your eye is beautiful" (it is because your eye is beautiful to see the beauty). This charming way of receiving and returning a compliment avoids the worry of envy and the need to pretend to offer the blouse. Instead, it appreciates the person who genuinely sees and values beauty in another.

Just as Jordanian Muslim women taught me this beautiful response, they can also teach each other that there's no need to envy others or fear receiving compliments. I believe Muslim women can embrace biblical truths that address envy and the evil eye within supportive communities. Together, they can cultivate a spirit of contentment and practice generosity born out of it. They can see the needs of others with compassionate and bountiful eyes instead of envious ones.

By doing so, they can move beyond envy and fear, embracing a path of grace and generosity that reflects God's abundant blessings. This is what it means to be an honorable woman. I long to walk this path together, encouraging and uplifting one another, pushing the spirit of envy away, and creating communities where grace and generosity flourish.

Bibliography

Abu Dawud. *English Translation of Sunan Abu Dawud*. Translated by Yaser Qadhi. Riyadh: Darussalam, 2008.

Abu-Rabia, Aref. "The Evil Eye and Cultural Beliefs Among the Bedouin Tribes of the Negev, Middle East." *Folklore* 116 (2005) 241–54.

Akkach, Samer, ed. *Naẓar: Vision, Belief, and Perception in Islamic Cultures*. Islamic History and Civilization 191. Leiden: Brill, 2022.

Algharabali, Nada, and Hanan Tagi. "Say Mashallah! Investigating Sociolinguistic Manifestations of the Evil Eye in Kuwait." *International Journal of Language and Culture* 7 (2020) 147–63.

Ali, Abdullah Yusuf. *The Glorious Qur'ān*. London: Islamic Foundation, 1975.

Allison, Dale C., Jr. *The Sermon on the Mount: Inspiring the Moral Imagination*. New York: Crossroad, 1999.

Al-Bukhārī, Muḥammad Ibn Ismāʿīl, and Muhammad Muhsin Khan. *Ṣaḥīḥ Al-Bukhārī: The Translation of the Meanings of Ṣaḥīḥ Al-Bukhārī*. 4th ed. 9 vols. Beirut: Dār Al-ʿArabīyah, 1985.

Al-Qurṭubi, Muḥammad Ibn Aḥmad. *Al-Jamiʿ Li-Aḥkam Al-Qurʾan*. 5th ed. Beirut: Dar Al-Kutub Al-Ilmiyah, 1996.

Al-Razi, Fakhr Al-Din Muḥammad Ibn Umar, and Aḥmad Shams Al-Din. *Al-Tafsīr Al-Kabīr, Aw, Mafatiḥ Al-Ghayb*. Beirut: Dar Al-Kutub Al-Ilmiyah, 1990.

Al-Ṭayalisi, Abi Dawud. *The Musnad of Abi Dawud al Tayalisi*. Beirut: Dar al-Kitab al-Lubnani, 1980.

Ammar, Hamed. *Growing Up in an Egyptian Village: Silwa, Province of Aswan*. London: Routledge and Kegan Paul, 1954.

An-Nasai, Ahmad. "The Book of Seeking Refuge with Allah." Sunnah, n.d. From *Sunan an-Nasa'i*, vol. 6, bk. 50, Hadith 5496. https://sunnah.com/nasai:5494.

Apostolides, Anastasia, and Yolanda Dreyer. "The Greek Evil Eye, African Witchcraft, and Western Ethnocentrism." *HTS Theological Studies* 64 (2008) 1021–42. https://doi.org/10.4102/hts.v64i2.39.

Arberry, Arthur J. *The Koran Interpreted*. New York: Touchstone, 1995.

Asad, Muhammad. *The Message of the Qurʾan*. London: Dar Al-Andalus, 1980.

BIBLIOGRAPHY

Bailey, Clinton. "Bedouin Religious Practices in Sinai and the Negev." *Anthropos* 77 (1982) 65–88.

Barclay, William. *The Letters to the Galatians and Ephesians.* 3rd ed. New Daily Study Bible. Louisville: Westminster John Knox, 2002.

Ben-Amos, Dan. "Toward a Definition of Folklore in Context." *Journal of American Folklore* 84 (1971) 3–15. https://www.jstor.org/stable/539729.

Binde, Per. *Bodies of Vital Matter: Notions of Life Force and Transcendence in Traditional Southern Italy.* Gothenburg Studies in Social Anthropology 14. Göteborg, Swed.: Gothenburg University Press, 1999. https://gupea.ub.gu.se/bitstream/handle/2077/29000/gupea_2077_29000_1.pdf?sequence=1.

Bledsoe, David Allen. "Evil Eye: Ancient, Yet Contemporary Phenomenon and a Biblical Response." *Evangelical Missions Quarterly* 49 (2013) 404–10.

Bridges, Carl B., and Ronald E. Wheeler. "The Evil Eye in the Sermon on the Mount." *Stone-Campbell Journal* 4 (2001) 69–79.

Budge, E. A. Wallis. *Amulets and Superstitions.* Oxford: Oxford University Press, 1930.

Chrysostom, John. "*Commentary on the Epistle to the Galatians*" and "*Homilies on the Epistle to the Ephesians.*" Translated by members of the English Church. Oxford: Parker, 1840.

Cole, R. Alan. *Galatians.* 2nd ed. TNTC 9. Nottingham: IVP Academic, 2008.

Cox, Marian R. *An Introduction to Folk-Lore.* London: Nutt, 1895.

Cullman, Oscar. *The Earliest Christian Confessions.* Translated by J. K. S. Reid. London: Lutterworth, 1949.

Cunningham, Graham. *Deliver Me from Evil: Mesopotamian Incantations 2500–1500 BC.* StPohl 17. Rome: Pontifical Bible Institute Press, 2007.

Daniels, Gene, and Warrick Farah, eds. *Margins of Islam: Ministry in Diverse Muslim Contexts.* Pasadena: Carey, 2018.

Davies, W. D., and Dale C. Allison, Jr. *The Gospel According to St. Matthew.* 3 vols. ICC. Edinburgh: T&T Clark, 1988.

deSilva, David A. *The Letter to the Galatians.* NICNT. Grand Rapids: Eerdmans, 2018.

Dickie, Matthew W. "Heliodorus and Plutarch on the Evil Eye." *Classical Philology* 86 (1991) 17–29. http://www.jstor.org/stable/270070.

Donaldson, Bess Allen. "The Evil Eye in Iran." In *The Evil Eye: A Casebook*, edited by Alan Dundes, 66–77. Madison: University of Wisconsin Press, 1992.

Douglas, Mary. *Witchcraft Confessions and Accusations.* Anthropology and Ethnography. London: Routledge, 1970.

Dundes, Alan. *The Evil Eye: A Casebook.* Madison: University of Wisconsin Press, 1992.

———. "Wet and Dry, the Evil Eye: An Essay in Indo-European and Semitic Worldview." In *The Evil Eye: A Casebook*, edited by Alan Dundes, 257–312. Madison: University of Wisconsin Press, 1992.

Eickelman, Dale F. "The Study of Islam in Local Contexts." *Journal of Developing Societies* 17 (1982) 1–16.

BIBLIOGRAPHY

Elliott, John H. *Beware the Evil Eye: The Evil Eye in the Bible and the Ancient World.* 4 vols. Eugene, OR: Cascade, 2017.

———. "Envy, Jealousy, and Zeal in the Bible: Sorting out the Social Differences and Theological Implications—No Envy for YHWH." In *To Break Every Yoke: Essays in Honor of Marvin L. Chaney*, edited by Robert B. Coote and Norman K. Gottwald, 344–64. SWBA, 2nd ser., 3. Sheffield, Eng.: Sheffield Phoenix, 2007.

———. "The Evil Eye and the Sermon on the Mount: Contours of a Pervasive Belief in Social Scientific Perspective." *BibInt* 2 (1994) 51–84.

———. "Paul, Galatians, and the Evil Eye." *CurTM* 17 (1990) 262–73.

———. "Social-Scientific Criticism: Perspective, Process and Payoff; Evil Eye Accusation at Galatia as Illustration of the Method." *HTS Theological Studies* 67 (2011). http://hts.org.za/index.php/HTS.

Elster, Jon. "Envy in Social Life." In *Strategy and Choice*, edited by Richard J. Zeckhauser, 49–82. Cambridge, MA: MIT Press, 1991.

Elworthy, Frederick Thomas. *The Evil Eye: An Account of this Ancient and Widespread Superstition.* London: Murray, 1895.

Esler, Philip F. "The Mediterranean Context of Early Christianity." In *The Early Christian World*, edited by Philip F. Esler, 3–26. 2nd ed. Routledge Worlds. London: Routledge, 2017.

Evans-Pritchard, E. E. *Witchcraft, Oracles and Magic Among the Azande.* Abridged ed. Oxford: Oxford University Press, 1976.

Fensham, F. C. "The Good and Evil Eye in the Sermon on the Mount." *Neot* 1 (1967) 51–58.

Fiensy, David A. "The Importance of New Testament Background Studies in Biblical Research: The 'Evil Eye' in Luke 11:34 as a Case Study." *Stone-Campbell Journal* 2 (1999) 75–88.

Foster, George M. "The Anatomy of Envy: A Study in Symbolic Behavior." *Current Anthropology* 13 (1972) 165–202.

———. "Peasant Society and the Image of Limited Good." *American Anthropologist* 67 (1965) 293–315.

France, R. T. *The Gospel of Matthew.* NICNT. Grand Rapids: Eerdmans, 2007.

Galt, Anthony H. "The Evil Eye as Synthetic Image and Its Meanings on the Island of Pantelleria, Italy." *American Ethnologist* (1982) 664–81.

Gershman, Boris. "The Economic Origins of the Evil Eye Belief." *Journal of Economic Behavior and Organization* 110 (2015) 119–44.

———. "The Two Sides of Envy." *Journal of Economic Growth* 19 (2014) 407–38.

Ghosh, Amitav. "The Relations of Envy in an Egyptian Village." *Ethnology* 22 (1983) 211–23.

Gill, John. *Exposition of the Bible: Proverbs.* Bible Study Tools, n.d. https://www.biblestudytools.com/commentaries/gills-exposition-of-the-bible/proverbs/.

Hadaway, Robin Dale. *The Muslim Majority: Folk Islam and the Seventy Percent.* Nashville: B&H Academic, 2021.

Bibliography

Haleem, M. A. S. Abdel. *The Qur'an: A New Translation.* Oxford World's Classics. New York: Oxford University Press, 2004.

Hardie, Margaret M. "The Evil Eye in Some Greek Villages of the Upper Haliakmon Valley in West Macedonia." *Journal of the Royal Anthropological Institute of Great Britain and Ireland* 53 (1923) 160–72. https://www.jstor.org/stable/2843757.

Harfouche, Jamal Karam. "The Evil Eye and Infant Health in Lebanon." In *The Evil Eye: A Casebook*, edited by Alan Dundes, 86–106. Madison: University of Wisconsin Press, 1992.

Hargitai, Quinn. "The Strange Power of the Evil Eye." BBC, Feb. 19, 2018. https://www.bbc.com/culture/article/20180216-the-strange-power-of-the-evil-eye.

Hassan, Riaz. *Faithlines: Muslim Conceptions of Islam and Society.* Oxford Pakistan Paperbacks. Oxford: Oxford University Press, 2002.

Hendriksen, William. *Matthew.* Hendriksen New Testament Commentaries. Edinburgh: Banner of Truth, 1973.

Herzfeld, Michael. "Meaning and Morality: A Semiotic Approach to Evil Eye Accusations in a Greek Village." *American Ethnologist* 8 (1981) 560–74. https://doi.org/10.1525/AE.1981.8.3.02A00090.

Hiebert, Paul G. "Power Encounter and Folk Islam." In *Muslims and Christians on the Emmaus Road*, edited by J. Dudley Woodberry, 45–61. Monrovia, CA: MARC, 1989.

Hiebert, Paul G., et al. *Understanding Folk Religion: A Christian Response to Popular Beliefs and Practices.* Grand Rapids: Baker Academic, 1999.

Homer. *The Iliad.* Translated by M. S. Silk. Cambridge: Cambridge University Press, 1987.

Howell, David. "Health Rituals at a Lebanese Shrine." *Middle Eastern Studies* 6 (1970) 179–88.

Huffard, Evertt W. "Culturally Relevant Themes About Christ." In *Muslims and Christians on the Emmaus Road*, edited by J. Dudley Woodberry, 161–74. Monrovia, CA: MARC, 1989.

Ibn al-Hajjaj al-Naysaburi, Muslim. *Shahih al Muslim.* Sunnah, n.d. https://sunnah.com/muslim.

Ibn Hanbal, Ahmad. *English Translation of "Musnad Imam Ahmad bin Hanbal."* Translated by Nasiruddin Al-Khattab. 6 vols. Riyadh: Darussalam, 2012.

Ibn Kathīr, Abu Al-Fida Ismail. *Tafsir Ibn Kathir.* Abridged under the supervision of Safiur-Rahman Al-Mubarakpuri. 10 vols. Riyadh: Darussalam, 2003.

Idel, Moshe. "Foreword." In *Jewish Magic and Superstition: A Study in Folk Religion*, by Joshua Trachtenberg, xxvii–xxviii. Repr., Philadelphia: University of Pennsylvania Press, 2004.

Islam, F., and R. A. Campbell. "'Satan Has Afflicted Me!' Jinn-Possession and Mental Illness in the Qur'an." *Journal of Religion and Health* 53 (2014) 229–43. doi: 10.1007/s10943-012-9626-5.

Bibliography

Jacobsen, Frode F. "Context and Uncertainty in Narratives: Stories of Sickness Among the Beja of Northeastern Sudan." *Anthropology & Medicine* 19 (2012) 291–302.

———. "Interpretations of Sickness and Misfortune Among Beja Pastoralists." *Anthropology & Medicine* 5 (1998) 145–67.

Jahn, Otto. "Über den Aberglauben des bösen Blickes bei den Alten." In *Berichte der Sächsischen Gesellschaft der Wissenschaften zu Leipzig, Philologisch-Historische Classe*, 28–110 and 5 plates. Leipzig: Hirzel, 1855.

Jerome. *Commentary on Galatians*. Edited by David G. Hunter. Translated by Andrew Cain. Washington, DC: Catholic University of America Press, 2010.

Jones, Louis C. "Evil Eye Among European-Americans." In *The Evil Eye: A Casebook*, edited by Alan Dundes, 150–68. Madison: University of Wisconsin Press, 1992.

Keener, Craig S. *The Gospel of Matthew: A Social-Rhetorical Commentary*. Grand Rapids: Eerdmans, 2009.

Keener, Craig S., and John H. Walton. *NIV Cultural Backgrounds Study Bible: Bringing to Life the Ancient World of Scripture*. Grand Rapids: Zondervan, 2016.

Kidner, Derek. *The Proverbs: An Introduction and Commentary*. TOTC. Lisle, IL: Intervarsity, 1975.

Kim, Sam. "Identity Crisis of Jordanian BMB Women at the Beginning Phase of New Faith." PhD diss., Asbury Theological Seminary, 2013.

Knight, Michael Muhammad. *Magic in Islam*. New York: TarcherPerigee, 2016.

Koç, Bozkurt, and Akın Temür. "The Superstitious Mystery Behind the Eye: The Symbol of Eye and the Way that the Evil Eye Bead Is Reflected in Turkish Society from the Ancient History to the Present." *Journal of History School* 7 (2014) 11–50. https://doi.org/10.14225/joh496.

Kord, Susanne. "From Evil Eye to Poetic Eye: Witch Beliefs and Physiognomy in the Ages of Enlightenment." In *Practicing Progress: The Promise and Limitations of Enlightenment*, edited by Richard E. Schade and Dieter Sevin, 35–57. New York: Rodopi, 2007.

Larson, Warren. "Ordinary Muslims and the Gospel." In *Margins of Islam: Ministry in Diverse Muslim Contexts*, edited by Gene Daniels and Warrick Farah, 81–92. Pasadena: Carey, 2018.

Lee, Dae-Young. "Developing Principles for Medical Missions in the Arab World in Light of the Biblical Concept of Shalom." PhD diss., Columbia International University, 2019.

Levin, S. "The Evil Eye and the Afflictions of Children." *South African Medical Journal* (1958) 663–65.

Lykiardopoulos, Amica. "The Evil Eye: Towards an Exhaustive Study." *Folklore* 92 (1981) 221–30.

Lightfoot, Joseph B. *Saint Paul's Epistle to the Galatians*. 3rd ed. London: Macmillan, 1869.

BIBLIOGRAPHY

Livingstone, Greg. *Planting Churches in Muslim Cities: A Team Approach.* Grand Rapids: Baker, 1993.

Love, Rick. "Church Planting Among Folk Muslims." *IJFM* 11 (1994) 87–91.

———. *Muslims, Magic, and the Kingdom of God: Church Planting Among Folk Muslims.* Pasadena: Carey, 2000.

Lutfiyya, Abdulla M. *Baytin: A Jordanian Village.* The Hague: Mouton & Co., 1966.

MacArthur, John. *Matthew 1–7.* MacArthur New Testament Commentary. Chicago: Moody, 1985.

Malina, Bruce J. *The New Testament World: Insights from Cultural Anthropology.* 3rd ed. Louisville: Westminster John Knox, 2001.

Mallowan, M. E. L. "Excavations at Brak and Chagar Bazar." *IRAQ* 9 (1947) f1–f9.

Maloney, Clarence, ed. *The Evil Eye.* New York: Columbia University Press, 1976.

Maltby, Tammy, with Anne Christian Buchanan. *The God Who Sees You: Look to Him When You Feel Discouraged, Forgotten, or Invisible.* Rev. ed. Colorado Springs: Cook, 2012.

Manzakoğlu, Bilgen Tuncer, and Saliha Türkmenoğlu Berkan. "Evil Eye Belief in Turkish Culture: Myth of Evil Eye Bead." *Turkish Online Journal of Design, Art and Communication* 6 (2016) 193–204. http://dx.doi.org/10.7456/10602100/013.

McDaniel, Walton B. "The Pupula Duplex and Other Tokens of an 'Evil Eye' in the Light of Ophthalmology." *Classical Philology* 13 (1918) 335–46. https://www.journals.uchicago.edu/doi/pdf/10.1086/360189.

Migdadi, Fathi, et al. "Divine Will and Its Extensions: Communicative Functions of Maašaallah in Colloquial Jordanian Arabic." *Communication Monographs* 77 (2010) 480–99.

Migdadi, Fathi H. "Complimenting in Jordanian Arabic: A Socio-Pragmatic Analysis." PhD diss., Ball State University, 2003.

Migliore, Sam. *Malúocchiu: Ambiguity, Evil Eye, and the Language of Distress.* Anthropological Horizons. Toronto: University of Toronto Press, 1997.

Moss, Candida R. "Blurred Vision and Ethical Confusion: The Rhetorical Function of Matthew 6:22–23." *CBQ* 73 (2011) 757–76.

Muller, Roland. *Honor and Shame: Unlocking the Door.* Bloomington, IN: Xlibris, 2000.

———. *The Messenger, the Message, and the Community.* Istanbul: CanBooks, 2006.

Mullick, Mohammad S. I., et al. "Beliefs About Jinn, Black Magic and Evil Eye in Bangladesh: The Effects of Gender and Level of Education." *Mental Health, Religion and Culture* 16 (2013) 719–29. https://doi.org/10.1080/13674676.2012.717918.

Musk, Bill. *The Unseen Face of Islam: Sharing the Gospel with Ordinary Muslims at Street Level.* Grand Rapids: Monarch, 2003.

Bibliography

Nasr, Seyyed Hossein, ed. *The Study Quran: A New Translation and Commentary*. New York: HarperOne, 2015.

Neyrey, Jerome H. "Bewitched in Galatia: Paul and Cultural Anthropology." *CBQ* 50 (1988) 72–100.

Nicholls, Ruth. "Popular Advice on Combatting Evil in Islam: Case Studies from Pakistan." In *Insights into Sufism: Voices from the Heart*, edited by Ruth J. Nicholls and Peter G. Riddell, 86–106. Newcastle upon Tyne, Eng.: Cambridge Scholars, 2020.

Nuño, Antón Alvar. "Ocular Pathologies and the Evil Eye in the Early Roman Principate." *Numen* 59 (2012) 295–321. https://doi.org/10.1163/156852712X641769.

Okka, Berrin, et al. "Traditional Practices of Konya Women During Pregnancy, Birth, the Postpartum Period, and Newborn Care." *Turkish Journal of Medical Sciences* 46 (2016) 501–11.

Omran, Roohallah Mohamad Alinejad. "Recognizing the Legitimacy of Evil Eye from the Perspective of Quran, Narrations and Medical Knowledge." *Journal of Quran and Medicine* 5 (2021) 49–58.

Oyler, D. S. "The Shilluk's Belief in the Evil Eye." *Sudan Notes and Records* 2 (1919) 122–37.

Padwick, Constance E. "Notes on the Jinn and the Ghoul in the Peasant Mind of Lower Egypt." *Bulletin of the School of Oriental Studies* 3 (1924) 421–46.

Park, Roswell. *The Evil Eye: Thanatology and Other Essays*. Boston: Gorham, 1912.

Parshall, Phil. *Bridges to Islam: A Christian Perspective on Folk Islam*. Grand Rapids: Baker, 1991.

———. *Inside the Community: Understanding Muslims Through Their Traditions*. Grand Rapids: Baker, 1994.

Pfeiffer, Charles F., and Everett F. Harrison, eds. *The New Testament and Wycliffe Bible Commentary*. New York: Moody Monthly, 1961.

Pickthall, Mohammed Marmaduke. *The Meaning of the Glorious Koran: An Explanatory Translation*. New York: Dorset, 1980.

Pierce, Joe E. *Life in a Turkish Village: Case Studies in Cultural Anthropology*. Edited by George Spindler and Louise Spindler. New York: Holt, Rinehart and Winston, 1964.

Pilch, John J. *Healing in the New Testament: Insights from Medical and Mediterranean Anthropology*. Minneapolis: Fortress, 2000.

Pliny the Elder. *Natural History*. 10 vols. Translated by H. Rackham. LCL. Cambridge, MA: Harvard University Press, 1969.

Plutarch. *Plutarch's "Moralia."* Edited by E. H. Warmington. Translated by Paul A. Clement and Herbert B. Hoffleit. LCL. Cambridge, MA: Harvard University Press, 1969.

Pócs, Éva. "Evil Eye in Hungary: Belief, Ritual, Incantation." In *Charms and Charming in Europe*, edited by Jonathan Roper, 205–27. London: Palgrave Macmillan, 2004.

Potts, Albert M. *The World's Eye*. Lexington: University Press of Kentucky, 1982.

BIBLIOGRAPHY

Qamar, Azher Hameed. "Belief in the Evil Eye and Early Childcare in Rural Punjab, Pakistan." *Asian Ethnology* 75 (2016) 397–418.

———. "The Concept of the 'Evil' and the 'Evil Eye' in Islam and Islamic Faith-Healing Traditions." *Journal of Islamic Thought and Civilization* 3 (2013) 44–53.

Rahman, Hamidi Abdul, and Supyan Hussin. "Case Study of Using Ruqyah Complementary Therapy on a British Muslim Patient with Cluster Headache." *European Journal of Medical and Health Sciences* 3 (2021) 5–7.

Rassool, G. Hussein. *Evil Eye, Jinn Possession, and Mental Health Issues: An Islamic Perspective.* London: Routledge, 2019.

Rayan, Ahmad, and Mirna Fawaz. "Cultural Misconceptions and Public Stigma Against Mental Illness Among Lebanese University Students." *Perspectives in Psychiatric Care* 54 (2017) 1–8. https://doi.org/10.1111/ppc.12232.

Redfield, Robert. *"The Little Community" and "Peasant Society and Culture."* Midway Reprint. Chicago: University of Chicago Press, 1989.

Reisacher, Evelyne A. "Who Represents Islam?" In *Margins of Islam: Ministry in Diverse Muslim Contexts*, edited by Gene Daniels and Warrick Farah, 1–11. Pasadena: Carey, 2018.

Reisacher, Evelyne A., et al., eds. *Toward Respectful Understanding and Witness Among Muslims: Essays in Honor of J. Dudley Woodberry.* Pasadena: Carey, 2012.

Reminick, Ronald A. "The Evil Eye Belief Among the Amhara." In *The Evil Eye*, edited by Clarence Maloney, 85–101. New York: Columbia University Press, 1976.

Roberts, John M. "Belief in the Evil Eye in World Perspective." In *The Evil Eye*, edited by Clarence Maloney, 223–78. New York: Columbia University Press, 1976.

Rodkinson, Michael L. *History of Amulets, Charms and Talismans: A Historical Investigation into Their Nature and Origin.* New York: N.p., 1893.

Roussou, Eugenia. "Orthodoxy at the Crossroads: Popular Religion and Greek Identity in the Practice of the Evil Eye." *Journal of Mediterranean Studies* 20 (2011) 85–105. https://muse.jhu.edu/pub/303/article/671923/summary#info_wrap.

Sanchez, Alberto Ruy. "The Hand of Fatima: Silent and Tactile." *Artes de Mexico*, Mayo 131 (2019) 84–86. https://www.jstor.org/stable/10.2307/26926769.

Sanneh, Lamin. "Amulets and Muslim Orthodoxy." *International Review of Missions* 63 (1974) 515–29.

Savage-Smith, Emilie, ed. *Magic and Divination in Early Islam.* Formation of the Classical Islamic World. Aldershot, Eng.: Ashgate, 2004.

Sayed, Nafisa Ali. "The Hand of Hamsa: Interpretation Across the Globe." *Research on Humanities and Social Sciences* 6 (2016) 23–26. https://core.ac.uk/download/pdf/234675429.pdf.

Schimmel, Annemarie. *Mystical Dimensions of Islam.* Chapel Hill: University of North Carolina Press, 1975.

BIBLIOGRAPHY

Schoeck, Helmut. *Envy: A Theory of Social Behaviour*. Indianapolis: Liberty, 1987.

———. "The Evil Eye: Forms and Dynamics of a Universal Superstition." In *The Evil Eye: A Casebook*, edited by Alan Dundes, 192–200. Madison: University of Wisconsin Press, 1992.

Schreiner, Thomas R. *Galatians*. Edited by Clinton E. Arnold. Zondervan Exegetical Commentary on the New Testament. Grand Rapids: Zondervan, 2010.

Smith, Marian W. "Village Notes from Bengal." *American Anthropologist* 48 (1946) 574–92.

Smith, Richard H., and S. H. Kim. "Comprehending Envy." *Psychological Bulletin* 133 (2007) 46–64.

Spence, Samantha. *Witchcraft Accusations and Persecutions as a Mechanism for the Marginalisation of Women*. Newcastle upon Tyne, Eng.: Cambridge Scholars, 2017.

Spoer, H. Henry. "Arabic Magic Medicinal Bowls." *Journal of the American Oriental Society* 55 (1935) 237–56.

Spooner, Brian. "The Evil Eye in the Middle East." In *The Evil Eye*, edited by Clarence Maloney, 311–20. New York: Columbia University Press, 1976.

Stacey, Vivienne. *Christ Supreme over Satan: Spiritual Warfare, Folk Religion and the Occult*. Lahore: Masihi Ishaát Khana, 1986.

———. "Power Encounters when Ministering to Muslim Women." Zwemer Center for Muslim Studies, n.d. https://www.zwemercenter.com/power-encounters/.

Staples, W. E. "Muhammad, a Talismanic Force." *American Journal of Semitic Languages and Literatures* 57 (1940) 63–70.

Stein, Howard F. "Envy and the Evil Eye Among Slovak-Americans: An Essay in the Psychological Ontology of Belief and Ritual." *Ethos* 2 (1974)15–46.

Stephenson, Peter H. "Hutterite Belief in Evil Eye: Beyond Paranoia and Towards a General Theory of Invidia." *Culture, Medicine and Psychiatry* 3 (1979) 247–65.

Story, William W. "*Castle St. Angelo*" *and "The Evil Eye": Being Additional Chapters to "Roba di Roma."* London: Chapman and Hall, 1877.

Strong, Cynthia A., and Meg Page, eds. *A Worldview Approach to Ministry Among Muslim Women*. Pasadena: Carey, 2006.

Thompson, R. Campbell. *The Devils and Evil Spirits of Babylonia*. 2 vols. Repr., Cambridge: Cambridge University Press, 2018.

Thomsen, Marie-Louise. "The Evil Eye in Mesopotamia." *JNES* 51 (1992)19–32.

Thomsen, Marie-Louise, and Frederick H. Cryer. *Witchcraft and Magic in Europe*. Vol. 1 of *Biblical and Pagan Societies*. London: Athlone, 2001.

Tolmie, D. Francois. *Persuading the Galatians: A Text-Centered Rhetorical Analysis of a Pauline Letter*. WUNT, 2nd ser., 190. Tübingen: Mohr Siebeck, 2005.

Trachtenberg, Joshua. *Jewish Magic and Superstition: A Study in Folk Religion*. Philadelphia: University of Pennsylvania Press, 2004.

Bibliography

Turner, David L. *Matthew.* BECNT. Grand Rapids: Baker Academic, 2008.
Ulmer, Rivka. *The Evil Eye in the Bible and in Rabbinic Literature.* Hoboken: KTAV, 1994.
Valletta, Nicola. *Cicalata sul Fascino, volgarmente detto Jettatura.* Naples: Gennaro Reale, 1818.
Van Rheenen, Gailyn. *Communicating Christ in Animistic Contexts.* Pasadena: Carey, 1991.
Vidaillet, Bénédicte. *Workplace Envy.* New York: Palgrave Macmillan, 2008.
Wazana, Nili. "A Case of the Evil Eye: Qohelet 4:4–8." *JBL* 126 (2007) 685–702.
Westermarck, Edward. *Ritual and Belief in Morocco.* 2 vols. London: Macmillan, 1926.
Wilson, M. Brett. "The Failure of Nomenclature: The Concept of 'Orthodoxy' in the Study of Islam." *Comparative Islamic Studies* 3 (2007) 169–94. https://journal.equinoxpub.com/CIS/article/view/9318.
Wright, Christopher J. H. *Deuteronomy.* New International Biblical Commentary. Peabody, MA: Hendrickson, 1996.
Wurmser, Léon, and Heidrun Jarass, eds. *Jealousy and Envy: New Views About Two Powerful Feelings.* New York: Analytic, 2011.
Zizzo, Daniel. "The Cognitive and Behavioral Economics of Envy." In *Envy: Theory and Research,* edited by R. H. Smith, 190–210. Affective Science. Oxford: Oxford University Press, 2008.
———. "Fear the Evil Eye." Department of Economics Discussion Paper 91. University of Oxford, 2002. https://ora.ox.ac.uk/objects/uuid:572c5913-7a34-4b71-97c7-2b5e715d354a.
Zwemer, Samuel. *The Influence of Animism on Islam: An Account of Popular Superstitions.* New York: Macmillan, 1920.

www.ingramcontent.com/pod-product-compliance
Lightning Source LLC
Chambersburg PA
CBHW071217160426
43196CB00012B/2335